Dedicated

to the following congregations:

The First Baptist Church, Greenwood, South Carolina

The Myers Park Baptist Church, Charlotte, North Carolina

The Warrenton Baptist Church, Warrenton, North Carolina

The Mars Hill Baptist Church, Mars Hill, North Carolina

The Olin T. Binkley Memorial Baptist Church,
Chapel Hill, North Carolina

"WHITES ONLY"
A Pastor's Retrospective on Signs of the New South
Copyright © 1991
Judson Press, Valley Forge, PA 19482-0851
All rights reserved. No part of this publication may be reproduced, stored in a retrieval system, or transmitted in any form or by any means, electronic, mechanical, photocopying, recording, or otherwise, without the prior permission of the copyright owner, except for brief quotations included in a review of the book.

Quotations of the Bible are from
The Holy Bible, King James Version.
New Revised Standard Version of the Bible, copyrighted 1989 by the Division of Christian Education of the National Council of the Churches of Christ in the United States of America, and used by permission. All rights reserved.
Revised Standard Version of the Bible, copyrighted 1946, 1952, © 1971, 1973 by the Division of Christian Education of the National Council of the Churches of Christ in the U.S.A., and used by permission.

Top cover photograph used with permission from Magnum photos by Erwitt; bottom photograph by Karen A. Hamburg.

Library of Congress Cataloging-in-Publication Data
Seymour, Robert E. (Robert Edward), 1925–
    Whites only : a pastor's retrospective on signs of the new South/
by Robert E. Seymour, Jr.
        p.   cm.
    Includes bibliographical references.
    ISBN 0-8170-1178-1
    1. Seymour, Robert E. (Robert Edward), 1925– .   2. Baptists—
United States—Clergy—Biography.   3. Race Relations—Religious
aspects—Christianity.   4. Southern States—Race relations.
I. Title.
BX6495.S43A3 1991
261.8′348′0092—dc20
[B]   91-26372
                                                              CIP

The name JUDSON PRESS is registered as a trademark in the U.S. Patent Office.
Printed in the U.S.A.

Contents

Foreword

The Reverend Dr. Robert E. Seymour, Jr., now the retired pastor of the Olin T. Binkley Memorial Baptist Church of Chapel Hill, North Carolina, entered the Divinity School of Yale University in September 1945. He readily discovered how awkward and unrehearsed he was for the "Yankee" culture, as a transplant from a small mill town in South Carolina. He was most unprepared to see whites serving food to blacks and to be using showers next to blacks in the dormitory bathrooms. I entered the Divinity School Quadrangle at Yale at the very same time, as a beginning Ph.D. student, and I was one of the blacks he found there.

A few months ago I had the pleasure of having *My Moral Odyssey* published by Judson Press. It is a chronicle of my moral and social maturation as a black minister and educator, beginning in the Huntersville section of Norfolk, Virginia, in the early 1920s. Seymour illuminates the same corridor of social and political experience, shedding new light on this sojourn as a "liberal" white Southern Baptist pastor, spanning the same seven decades. His perspective is from one side of the railroad tracks; mine from the other.

I have known and appreciated Bob Seymour's committed career in ministry since I first learned of his call to the new Chapel Hill congregation in the 1950s. All blacks who were careful observers of our allies across the South knew of Clarence Jordan, Charles Jones, Carlyle Marney, Bob Seymour, and a few more. And we knew what a lonesome road they took with stead-fast devotion. We also knew of the shameful resistance they confronted at the hands of pious conformists who distorted their calling to ministry in the name of the unjust status quo.

In this book, Bob Seymour has provided for clergy and lay-persons one of the most authentic accounts yet written of the social metamorphosis in our nation. *"Whites Only"* is a candid chronicle of the changes that have taken place in America for which we are all grateful. It is a record also of the stubborn and recalcitrant nature of racism, and of the perpetual consequences of 244 years of slavery.

Once again we see persons like Rosa, Uncle Henry, Aunt Ada, and other loyal and dutiful blacks who were deeply loved by their white "families." After sixty years of care and devotion, Rosa appears at Bob Seymour's retirement; later, Bob unhesitat-ingly makes the trip from Chapel Hill to Rosa's bedside in Green-wood. Such incidents are a legitimate and factual part of the best of the South's cultural love from a time not too long—and not completely—past. One has to be gratified to observe that Bob Seymour could share in that diversion of southern tenderness and still fight for the dismantling of racial segregation, for equal education, fair housing, decent health care, and for qualified persons in public office. In that regard, he left countless of his contemporaries way behind.

He faced the raw reality of the emergence of "Black Power" and "Black Nationalism," developments that many liberal whites flinched at seeing. He became the target of some of that strange rhetoric from black pastors whom he thought he knew so well, and whose behavior he thought he could predict. But he did not resign in anger or contempt. He kept his vision of a great com-munity in plain view and stayed his course. Even in the reversals of the 1980s, he continued to rejoice at the new victories for justice, equality, and true community appearing slowly on the horizon. Because of Bob Seymour's long and tireless labors, there will be many more victories to celebrate in the pursuit of genuine community in our land.

Samuel D. Proctor
July 1991

Preface

William Faulkner once said, "The past is never dead; it's not even past." This judgment seems especially true of the South. The past keeps intruding. Even though things may never be quite the same again, the long shadow of memory makes it difficult to welcome the future wholeheartedly. This book is about a yesterday that will not completely release us and a tomorrow that never fully arrives.

What follows is not an autobiography in the usual sense. It is about a time and a place in history. It is an account of how one life was touched and shaped by the racial revolution in the American South. It represents a slow process of sorting memories, clippings, letters, and excerpts from old sermons. It is an attempt to show how one person, who felt called to be a pastor, navigated a stormy period of southern history with atypical beliefs that soon became second nature.

This is not a researched document. It is more in the genre of oral history. It is a retrospective by one who still feels deeply southern and yet is profoundly glad that the Old South is no more.

The record of the civil rights movement's strong base of support in the black churches of the South is well known, but little has been written about the responses of white congregations caught in the surrounding conflict. This book adds another piece to the mosaic of that troubled time and tells how established white churches dealt with the protracted controversy. It reports how several very different North Carolina congregations responded to the racial revolution.

In the final years of this century, many individuals who helped bring the New South into being will pass from the scene. "Story theology" claims that everyone has a personal history worth preserving. This book is one such story. It is offered to further the ongoing process of putting a most painful period in southern life into sharper focus.

Although the preferred use of the title "black" in reference to Negroes did not enter common parlance until the civil rights movement was well under way, I have taken the liberty of using both these terms interchangeably in recounting events prior to the 1960s.

I am indebted to many persons, including the members of my own family, for encouraging me to write these reflections on the past. The memories recorded here are not meant to be a memoir but are offered as an eyewitness commentary on a period of vast social change.

I acknowledge the helpful assistance of John Ehle's book *The Free Men* (New York: Harper and Row, 1965) as I sought to reconstruct the sequence of events in Chapel Hill's racial conflict. Also, special appreciation is due to Karen Elder and John Humber for their careful reading and critique of the text.

The many references to the Olin T. Binkley Memorial Baptist Church in the latter half of the book are in no sense intended to be a history of the extensive and creative ministries of that remarkable congregation.

Introduction

Statistics show that blacks who live outside the South are returning now at a steadily increasing rate. A reverse migration has begun. Blacks, who had left the region like Egyptian slaves journeying to the Promised Land, are coming back to freedom. Segregation has gone, and the New South offers a broad range of economic opportunity. It is also perceived as a more hospitable place.

Some blacks are heading back South to reclaim their family roots, but most are making the move because they believe the quality of life is better. Past oppression has been routed by voter registration, school desegregation, and enforceable laws against discrimination on the job. Many older blacks are returning to their homeland to retire.

Sociologists predict that this population resettlement pattern will continue for the foreseeable future. Southern blacks and whites are forging a new coalition around a widening democratic base. Everyone is assured a voice in shaping a destiny that will be shared by all.

Of course this does not mean that racism is dead, but now there is better protection against it. Blacks who fled North to escape prejudice soon learned that prejudice is a national phenomenon. It is by no means peculiar to the South, but the climate of mutual respect and acceptance may be improving faster in the South than anywhere else in the nation.

Southern people are more likely to experience face-to-face,

day-to-day relationships with persons of another race. Thousands of blacks, both in small towns and cities, now hold municipal offices. In the South people have always worked together, only now the workplace is changing. Instead of in cotton fields, it is behind the counter or in the classroom or at the next desk or side by side on the assembly line.

The Ku Klux Klan has suffered an almost fatal blow from recent court claims against its assets. The occasional violence that continues to erupt does not represent a rise in racism but, rather, the death rattle of a dying segregationist culture.

I was deeply moved when I saw the stage play *Driving Miss Daisy*. The play depicts a white-black relationship typical of the Old South. An aging woman and her chauffeur develop a touching friendship. As the drama develops, you see how much they care for each other, but whatever goodwill exists has to be expressed within the well-defined structures of segregation.

When I saw the play, I was sitting behind a sophisticated-looking black couple, and as I looked over their shoulders to the stage, I felt the sharp contrast between the past and the present. I experienced almost uncontrollable emotion as I recalled so many similar interracial friendships from my own South Carolina upbringing. I thought of Grandfather and his elderly hired man. I remembered my mother and her lifelong maid. Surreptitiously, I wiped away tears every time the house lights came up.

At the end of the play, the woman sitting next to me said, "I've seen this play five times."

I responded by conjecturing, "Then you must be from the South, too?"

But she was not from the South; she had always lived in the North. Then I added, "Well, my roots are in the South, and I've seen many such relationships in my time. To be sure, they were diseased relationships, but the people really cared for one another." The woman replied, "Better that kind of relationship than no relationship at all."

She may be right. Blacks in the North for the most part have lived at a distance from whites, whereas in the South the lives of both are bound up together. The good news is that these diseased relationships are amenable to healing. They can be replaced with healthy ones; the curse can be cured. Indeed, it is happening all across the Southland as members of both races leave the legacy of segregation behind. It is happening as surely as the seasons change, and no one can hold back the approaching spring.

We have passed through a period in American public education when references to religion have been kept to a minimum in textbooks because no one wanted to be accused of being partisan in matters of faith. We have not understood that it is impossible to understand American culture unless one sees the important place religion has had in our history. Although there is now an emerging consensus that such information in the curriculum does not compromise religious freedom nor the principle of separation of church and state, there is still a danger that future generations will not be taught that the civil rights movement began in the church. I hope we will keep alive the memory of Martin Luther King, Jr., as a preacher; indeed, as a Baptist preacher. Although the primary thrust of the racial revolution came out of the black church and not the white church, it was nonetheless the church.

Undoubtedly, the white church as an institution has suffered some loss of face for its failure to offer more courageous leadership in a time when it could have made such a great difference. Yet, that judgment should be balanced against the reality of the scattered church that permeated every southern community. Even when the gathered congregation kept silent, many southern Christians acted out their personal faith on the front line. Many shopkeepers, teachers, farmers, and professional folk were unsung heroes and heroines. David Garrow, an authority on the civil rights movement, who wrote the book *Bearing the Cross*, observes, "A balanced and inclusive telling of the civil rights story will make starkly clear how the transformation of the American South stemmed far more from direct involvement by thousands of relative unknowns than from the efforts of a few established organizations and prominent individuals."

Although Garrow had primary reference to the black community, the same judgment holds true for the white community. Those who made ugly headlines, the vicious and the violent, were in the minority; but the great majority, the kind and the caring, were also inconspicuously there. Even during the most stressful days of the racial struggle, goodwill from countless anonymous white Christians was a saving grace. These reservoirs of goodwill remain a continuing source of stability in the ongoing metamorphosis of the region.

❧

Many of the events recounted in the pages that follow will seem both timid and tame today, but at the time of their occurrence, much that was said and done was deemed highly controversial or radical to the extreme. This very fact is an impressive indication of how fast things have changed in the South and of the reality of the new inclusive society now emerging.

Even Eldridge Cleaver, the Black Panther civil rights leader who fled the United States to escape prosecution, as early as 1975 was quoted in the *New York Times* as saying, "With all its faults, the American politcal system is the freest and most democratic in the world."[1] Clearly, the system needs to be improved, but at last it is sufficiently open for all people with grievances to find political avenues for obtaining redress.

Surprisingly, there are few countries anywhere on earth today in which people are generally less prejudiced about color than Americans, the stereotypes of the Old South notwithstanding. This achievement can be accounted for to a significant degree because the racial isssue has always loomed so large in the national consciousness, as citizens have tried to close the gap between professed ideology and practice. Indeed, there are few places in the world where the racial issue looms so large as in the United States. The press is always alert to register offense in response to any careless ethnic slur made by a public figure. No doubt this very sensitivity to the issue insures steady progress toward removing those vestiges of prejudice that yet remain.

Chapter 1

Surviving a Revolution

When I turned and saw Rosa inching down the aisle as we sang the last hymn, I lost my composure. Until that moment I had experienced unexpected equanimity, with little of the heavy nostalgia I had feared would consume me. The retirement liturgy so successfully sounded a note of celebration that the pain was muted, but when I realized Rosa was there, an emotional upheaval proved irrepressible. I was not alone in my effort to suppress the tears; every member of my family wept with me.

At first I thought her presence was an arranged surprise. I assumed the planning committee had invited her and made possible her coming. The close of the service seemed a logical place for her to appear, and she was being escorted to the front of the sanctuary on the arm of an usher as if this were an intended part of the proceedings. So I arose to greet her and embraced her before the congregation. Then, without being fully aware of the symbolic truth of what I was about to say, I turned to the people now seated and announced, "This is my mother," presenting her.

In fact, as my mother's faithful maid for a generation, Rosa has been an alternate mother to me from almost the day of my birth. She came to work for "Miss Janie" when I was a preschooler, and ever since, she has been a part of my life, as if she were family.

I learned later that her presence at the retirement service was wholly self-initiated. She had heard about it from one of my relatives and had determined to attend. She persuaded a niece to drive the five-hour journey from Greenwood, leaving before dawn in order to get there by eleven for the morning worship service. They were a little late arriving, so an usher seated them on the very back row with Rosa next to himself. Of course he had no idea who she was until she began to punctuate the proceedings with a loud whisper, saying, "I raised him. I raised him!"

"You raised whom?" the usher finally asked.

"The preacher," she said, "the preacher." Spontaneously, the usher decided to lead her forward to the front of the sanctuary so the preacher would know she was there.

Rosa's appearance was an epiphany. Her presence became for me the precipitating event for this book. Suddenly, I saw my whole life linked to this simple, stately woman. For the first time, it struck me that my entire ministry—indeed, my very life—has been an extended commentary on the racial issue. The culture that nurtured me had been so completely conditioned by racial policy and prejudice that it shaped my life. Questioning exclusive racial practices and rebelling and protesting against them has demanded my primary attention from my first formative years to the conclusion of my professional career as a clergyman. As I looked back over the years at that moment when Rosa appeared, I realized she represented the thread of continuity in my life story. It was as if someone had pushed the playback button on my life. All at once, I could see how race, perhaps more than any other contingency, had set the agenda for my life.

Consider the contrast from the beginning until now. When Rosa first entered my life, we were both captive to a rigidly segregated South Carolina where all people, black and white alike, knew their places. Whereas today with the legal barriers to segregation down and the so-called New South emerging, I am a part of an innovative culture that is becoming increasingly inclusive. The South is changing so rapidly that it is often confusing and overwhelming for Rosa, for she remains illiterate and poor, still trapped in the legacy of racism.

We have survived a revolution, Rosa and I. Though skirmishes are still occurring and battles are yet to be fought, the region has changed so fast that the culture I live in today bears little resemblance to the Old South of my childhood. If someone had told me thirty years ago that such changes were ahead, I would have found it impossible to believe. I am convinced that nothing so far-reaching in its social impact, not imposed by a force of arms, has ever happened anywhere else in the world. A society once locked in a system of evil exploitation has experienced unparalleled liberation. Both people and structures have altered in unimaginable ways. And there is no turning back. Someone has judged that the tragedy of Rip Van Winkle was not that he slept twenty years but that he slept through a revolution. He slumbered undisturbed while battles raged all around him. When he finally woke up, he found himself living in quite a different world. Something similar to this has occurred in parts of the South where people have been slow to wake up to the reality of all that has happened. Now a new day is here, and the region, so often maligned and disdained by the rest of the nation, must be reckoned with as a land of great promise for all who live here, black and white alike. In Bruce Catton's account of the Civil War, *This Hallowed Ground*, he speaks of the inevitable, incalculable victory seeded by the admission of a common humanity. He writes,

> Negroes were in some inexplicable manner what the war itself was mostly about. Their status seemed mysteriously to be changing, and as it changed—if it changed—there must be corresponding changes in each of the social levels that lay above, and finally in the very way Americans looked upon their fellow human beings. For the most fundamental change of all was that it was becoming necessary to look upon the Negro as a man rather than a thing. Let that once take hold, and racism in all its forms must receive a mortal wound, even though it might be a very long time dying. What was won for the least of these would finally be won for everybody; and once a common humanity was admitted, an incalculable victory would have been gained, because sooner or later the admission would have to be acted upon.[1]

Catton's prophetic statement is an accurate assessment of all that has ensued and all we now see in progress. Decisive action has taken place at every level of our corporate life. The relationship between the races has improved so significantly in recent decades that today's young people are incredulous when told that at one time twin water fountains were installed to serve Negroes and whites separately. Indeed, it is hard for those of us who witnessed a march on Washington by 250,000 citizens to believe it was ever necessary to protest such entrenched racial injustice. Blacks were denied every basic right: to vote in any election, to work at any job, to live in a decent home in any neighborhood, to have access to schools, restaurants, hotels, theaters, restrooms, and even churches.

How far we have come! Obviously, there is still a great distance to go, but I have no patience with those who play down the progress achieved to date as if nothing has changed. Now blacks serve in high government positions; laws protect open housing, employment and all public accommodations. No, the American South is not yet a utopia, and it may never be, but in light of the recent history of its racially ruptured society, there is every reason for just pride in what it is rapidly becoming.

Martin Luther King, Jr., reminded the country repeatedly that the architects of our republic who drafted the Constitution, the Bill of Rights, and the Declaration of Independence were signing a promissory note to which every American would eventually fall heir. At last, that note has come due, guaranteeing inalienable rights to all.

Had America not risen up to begin living out the implications of its professed creed, the racial revolution surely would have been delayed at the cost of far more violence and death. The South African novelist, Alan Paton, once said of the incendiary situation in his country that his greatest fear was that by the time white people have turned to loving, blacks will have turned to hating. We have been exceedingly fortunate in the United States to have avoided bloodshed on every street and to have achieved so much by peaceful, nonviolent means.

The white people of this country owe an enormous debt of gratitude to black Americans for their never having lost faith in this land, for their continuing to believe—despite daily evidence to the contrary—that someday America would live up to its cherished ideals. Their patience and perseverance enabled them to survive against great odds and remain impressive testimonies to a stalwart people. They refused to allow their plight to eclipse hope or to give up on the government that oppressed them.

When asked by a foreign journalist why communism had failed to win much of a following among Negroes in America, a man replied, "It's bad enough being ostracized for being black, let alone for being black and red at the same time!" The fact is that other political philosophies never flourished here because blacks considered themselves Americans, too, and they looked forward to their eventual admission to mainstream citizenship.

Symptomatic of the unswerving commitment of blacks is the account of what happened in Montgomery, Alabama, on that terrible night when King's home was bombed during the bus boycott. While shouts of anger and the noise of sirens filled the air, a group of Negro women, huddled together on the front lawn, could be heard singing "My Country 'Tis of Thee."

These were God-fearing folk who had been taught not to hate. We must never forget that the civil rights movement began among religious people, men and women who were a part of the church. The church has not always been given due credit for its crucial role in the racial revolution. Although the black church was more vocal and visible throughout the struggle, the involvement of white congregations should not be discounted. The role of the white minister in many southern communities was a decisive influence in determining the nature of the response. Both in its corporate and individual member expressions, the church was a pervasive presence for good.

Although the civil rights revolution has affected the whole nation, it is in the South where the change has been most dramatic and continues steadily forward. In fact, there is convincing evidence that the South is making more progress in racial relationships than anywhere else in the country. Once the scapegoat of the nation, the South is rapidly becoming the showplace of the nation. When Boston was mandated to integrate its public schools by implementing a bus plan, they sent administrators to Charlotte, North Carolina, to learn how southerners did it so well.

Sustained progress in the South can be accounted for in part by the long experience of people of both races in living together on a day-by-day basis. Blacks and whites generally have resided in closer proximity to each other in the junctions and crossroads of Dixie than in the metropolitan centers of the North where de facto segregation has succeeded in keeping the races apart. Consequently, social interaction fosters integration more quickly in the South; members of both races have come together not as strangers but as persons who have always been on speaking terms. Whereas in the North integration was seen more as a philosophical objective with little personal experience upon which to base actual revolutionary change.

Integration is already far more evident in many southern towns than it may ever be elsewhere. All across the South, whites learned fast that the economic advancement of blacks was in everyone's best interest and made prosperity more likely for everybody. It finally became abundantly clear that in order to keep the black man in the ditch, the white man had to stay there with him to keep him in his place. Indeed, long-term self-interest, perhaps more than religious or moral suasion, accelerated the change. Business interests that were being harmed economically were often more ready to risk altering the system than were the politicians.

Fears once endemic are fast disappearing. Seeing blacks and whites together in nearly every conceivable situation is commonplace today. Government decrees accomplished this in state and federal agencies, and the weight of the law made it easy for businesses that had opposed opening their doors to blacks to do so while blaming their willingness on the Supreme Court. Public schools, long the nerve centers for social networking in southern communities, seem to be over the worst of the integration trauma. Though the educational level for the entire region is down, academic ratings are beginning to rise again. Some of the private schools founded to circumvent integration now find the cost of operation too high and are being forced to close. Some of the better ones that have survived now recruit promising black students to avoid being labeled racist.

I live in a town where only 15 percent of the population is black, but blacks are evident everywhere in its corporate life. The superintendent of the public schools is black. The district attorney is black. Blacks serve on the town board and the school board. The chair of the county commissioners is black. A black served as mayor for three terms, once uncontested. I do my banking with a black banker and watch a black newscaster every evening. I belong to a YMCA fitness center in nearby Durham where half the participants are black and where a cordial fraternal fellowship is taken for granted. Though the native black segment of the population still lives largely in one part of town, black newcomers are welcomed in every neighborhood.

Does this sound like the South? I must confess that I live in a university town, and what I have described is not altogether typical. Yet Chapel Hill was once as segregated as any other southern community, and I contend that what has happened here represents an ongoing process that will more and more become the regional norm.

Outside the South people often generalize about the region as if it were all of one piece, all the same. The fact is, there are many Souths. What is true of one community may not yet be true of another. What follows in these pages is a reflection upon a cross-section of the mid-South, from my South Carolina childhood to pastorates in western, central, and eastern North Carolina. In the mountains, there are few blacks; down East they are often the majority; and everywhere the impact of the racial revolution is evident. People of both races look to the future with mounting optimism and the hope of making it together.

After the Democratic Convention in Atlanta in 1988, Anthony Lewis wrote in the *New York Times*: "There is an ease of feeling here between black and white that is quite different from Boston or New York or Chicago. There, the least prejudiced person is still likely to feel a certain awareness, a self-consciousness in talking to someone of a different color. Here the courtesies, the attitudes seem to bridge race. And some southerners say human relationships are even easier elsewhere in the region, including Mississippi, than in Atlanta."[2]

Achievements of the racial revolution south of Mason-Dixon tend to be accepted as normal very quickly once they occur. Even an interracial marriage is accepted in stride in Chapel Hill. There is serious danger that the memory of the dark days of yesteryear when segregation reigned supreme will fade and that a new generation will not appreciate how far we have come. Soon the heroes and heroines of the sixties will be moving off the stage of history, many of them to remain nameless. The life stories and anecdotes of these countless unknown warriors in this protracted conflict will be lost forever.

In a recent address to the student body of the University of North Carolina, civil rights activist Julian Bond contended that those engaged in the continuing struggle sometimes act as if it had no history. He judged students to be "so ill-informed about landmark Supreme Court decisions as not to know what was changed by *Brown* v. *the School Board of Topeka* and to think that *Roe* v. *Wade* refers to alternate ways of crossing the Potomac." It is difficult for young people to believe that things could have been as bad as they were and that we have come so far.

Julian Bond is right. To forget the past is to risk losing what has been achieved at incalculable cost, as demonstrated by the Supreme Court's civil rights decisions during the Reagan years. Not to remember is an invitation to a relaxation of vigilance. Everyone stands to lose if the national consensus of conscience is allowed to erode.

As I commence my retirement years, I am experiencing the curious sensation of understanding myself better than ever before. I see clearly now that my primary goals and objectives throughout my career were shaped more by race than I ever

recognized previously. Yet, one thing I have known: I am a southerner, deeply rooted emotionally in this part of the world, and I
consider myself greatly blessed to have survived a revolution.
Never did I want to live or work anywhere else. When opportunities were offered to me to leave the region, I discovered I
could not consider them seriously; my ties were in the South, and
I could not sever them. I wanted to be engaged in what I saw
happening all around me, and I understood how important it was
for white people who were involved in the civil rights movement
to be from the South, to be able to speak to the situation from
within and not be vulnerable to that pejorative label "outsider."
Nothing has given to me a greater sense of destiny. Seldom
in history are persons given the opportunity to experience such
a strong sense of moral certitude about a righteous cause. There
was absolutely no question about the evil nature of the segregated society. It flagrantly contradicted the fundamentals of my
religious convictions and political philosophy. There has been
mounting exhilaration in this ongoing effort from those first
sit-ins in Greensboro, North Carolina, to the tumbling down of
all the "separate but equal" walls across the Southland. From the
outset, my commitment has been fired by the faith that God is
"trampling out the vintage where the grapes of wrath are stored."
God's truth is, indeed, "marching on."[3]

Chapter 2

Growing Up Southern

When I arrived at the segregated Greenwood County Hospital on that hot July day in 1925, my father telephoned other members of the family to announce excitedly, "We have a healthy baby boy, and his eyes are already open!" My father's rural upbringing had led to a mistaken assumption about infant humans.

My eyes were closed for a long time to the racial issue. When you are born into an established culture, you accept it as a given. I look back now and am appalled at how long it took me to begin questioning the separation of the races and to see the evil in the system. I am sure I remain blind to some of the realities of a racist society to this day, for the prejudicial conditioning of those first formative years left an indelible mark, never fully eradicated. I was carefully taught by both precept and example.

My family roots are deep in southern soil. Home is South Carolina, the first state to secede from the union to form the Confederacy. One grandfather came from Charleston; the other migrated from Mississippi to the Palmetto State after his own father was killed in the Civil War.

Greenwood was a small town at the turn of the century, but it grew rapidly as it became a major textile center. Negroes who came in from nearby farms to find work were confined to menial jobs in the mill, always the dirtiest and the most dangerous. The town became famous for the enlightened management policies of J.C. Self, who provided attractive brick houses for his people, meaning his white employees. Privileged executives were wryly tagged "Self-made men." I recall proudly touring the cotton mills with visitors at a time when I was totally insensitive to the paternalism and racism they represented.

My maternal grandfather came up the hard way, merchandising tin and coal, but finally he was given an opportunity to be on the ground floor of founding the local telephone company. This enabled him to rise to establishment status in the community and to build a large house on the edge of town that was surrounded by farm acreage with Negroes residing on the place. This was the setting into which I was born, an enclave with blacks and whites living in close proximity.

I do not remember much about Sadie when we lived at my grandfather's house, but she may be the black person who most affected my life because of what happened to my mother. Sadie was the cook at the big house and presided over a huge kitchen where stairs led down to a basement room in which my teetotaling grandfather made his own secret scuppernong wine. Sadie warned me that the boogie man lived down below and would get me if I didn't behave. She died of tuberculosis, but, before the disease was diagnosed, my mother was infected and later was repeatedly confined to bed for long periods during my childhood.

I have a better recollection of my grandfather's most faithful servant, known to all of us as simply Uncle Henry. We used his last name so seldom that I cannot even recall it. He and Aunt Ada lived a short walk down the hill from the home place. I knew them only in their aging years after their nine children had made an exodus North. I recall conversations among adults about several of their sons who had done well in Philadelphia. One was reported to be a postman. Whites would recount such success stories with subdued amazement, not simply because blacks so excelled, but rather, that whites would tolerate their holding such nontraditional jobs.

One of Uncle Henry's arms was severed just above the wrist. It never occurred to me to inquire how this had happened. Yet with remarkable dexterity, he continued to milk the cows and to set the fireplaces with wood every morning. He arrived at dawn as an almost ghostlike figure, entering and leaving the house unobtrusively.

Even as a child I understood that grandfather and Uncle Henry had a special kind of relationship. They were devoted to each other despite the distance that separated them. Granddaddy provided for Uncle Henry well, in a far better manner than most Negroes fared. His green frame house even boasted an indoor tub and toilet—by no means typical—and food was always shared. I recall taking generous plates of leftovers down the hill to Uncle Henry's house after many a sumptuous Sunday dinner.

Rosa entered my life when we moved from my grandfather's house into a new residence next door built by my parents. She lived immediately behind us in a traditional Negro cabin, not more than a hundred yards away. Rosa had two sons, Frank and James L., the first of eight children, the others yet to be born. They were my playmates until school age sent us our separate ways. The only thing I remember about those years is the derision directed against Frank for his slowness in learning how to speak. He would merely repeat the last word of what anyone said to him. Folk would deliberately bait him into talking and then laugh at his habit of echoing what was just said. Of course this taught me that blacks are not as smart as whites and that it is all right to make fun of their ineptness. Indeed, all racist humor reinforces the prejudice that black people are inferior.

I wonder now what Rosa's children might have become if they had had even half a chance at life. Frank ended up in the penitentiary and eventually disappeared when he was released. Recently, his brother returned home to die. He was debilitated with illness, a broken and impoverished man with nothing to show for his years. I stood by his bedside after more than a half-century separation, but we could find little to say to each other, no bridge of communication. After an awkward greeting, followed by a long silence heavy with nostalgia and sadness, we parted. I have been haunted by James L. ever since, for I feel as if I betrayed a friendship begun long ago as a child when I acquiesced to the social conventions of the only society I knew. For me, one opportunity led to another; but for him, life was programmed in narrow channels, a confinement that offered no choice but to conform.

How must all of this appear to Rosa? I cannot fathom what must surely be the conflicting emotions of a mother as she compares my career to that of her wayward sons. Even by her standards, Frank and James L. were ne'er-do-wells, yet she never seemed jealous or angry about the discrepancies in our life directions. She matter-of-factly judged her boys to be no good without ever blaming the system that predestined their failures and their fates. Her attitude suggests that she had been so brainwashed by the prejudicial judgments of southern culture that even she was convinced of the innate inferiority of her own sons.

Indoctrination in racial differences began for me from the day of my birth. When you are reared in a segregated society and never have occasion to see an alternative, you accept it as the way things are meant to be; indeed, as the very order of creation. White supremacy reigned supreme. As you learned the protocol, the system seemed to run smoothly and for the benefit of all. You become a victim of cultural osmosis from which there is no escape and no visible exception. When you grow up without ever seeing blacks in anything other than a servant class, you have difficulty believing they are capable of any other role or achievement. The reality of what *is* becomes a self-fulfilling prophecy of what is meant to be.

This is nowhere more evident than in the prevailing stereotypes that formed the mindset for rationalizing the legitimacy of segregation. All blacks were seen as Aunt Jemimas or Stepin Fetchits, a happy-go-lucky people who were basically simple but comfortable with their lot in life. Every negative trait for which they were credited was proved by a Catch-22 circumstance. They were proved limited in ability by being confined to menial jobs. They were proved dirty by being forced to live in filth and with inadequate sanitation. They were proved untruthful by learning that it was in their own best interest to tell the white man only what he wanted to hear. They were vulnerable to accusations of thievery when "toting" from the white lady's kitchen was the only way to provide sufficient food for their children. They were judged lazy while seldom challenged by meaningful work or when unemployed through no fault of their own.

A painful personal memory is the entertainment a cousin and I provided for nearly everyone in Greenwood. Someone taught us a song and dance routine, and wherever we were, people insisted that "Bo" and "Bet" perform "Shortnin' Bread." Always there was much merriment when we skipped forward and belted forth with exaggerated gestures, singing:

> Put on the skillet; put on the lid,
> Mama's gonna make a little shortnin' bread.
> Dat ain't all she's a gwinna do;
> she's a gonna make a little coffee, too.
> Mama's little baby loves shortnin' shortnin',

Mama's little baby loves shortnin' bread.
Two little darkies a lying in bed,
one of 'em sick and the other half dead.
Send fo' the doctor; the doctor said,
"Feed dem chillun on shortnin' bread!"

To have carried this dreadful ditty so clearly in my mind for over six decades constitutes convincing evidence of emotional child abuse. I was manipulated to entrench further the prejudicial stereotypes of those to whom my life had been entrusted. I judge it in retrospect to have been a criminal act, for now I feel a sense of humiliation as I recall my willing participation and pleasure at the vigorous applause.

I am sure my mother was party to this and saw it as something cute and totally innocent. She never would have hurt anyone willingly, black or white. Both my parents were prejudiced people, but they could never have seen themselves as such. Their self-image was that of folk who had the well-being of blacks at heart, protecting them as if they were children unable to take care of themselves. They honestly believed that the restrictions imposed upon blacks by the system were for their own good; segregation was the only conceivable arrangement for the races my parents could imagine. They were sincerely convinced it was the best way of life for all concerned, a kind of social contract offered by gracious whites to be gratefully accepted by dependent blacks. Southerners often said, "I'm for segregation the same way I'm a Baptist and a Democrat." It was all a part of the same creed, affirmed with incredible obliviousness to obvious contradictions.

The phrase "in their place" defined the parameters of black participation in the community. The boundary lines were clearly understood by members of both races. Any Negro who dared push beyond the limits was liable to punitive action that ranged all the way from arrest to vilification to being saddled with that most pejorative of labels, "an uppity nigger." Everything was separate and seldom, if ever, equal. Separate schools, hospitals, churches, restaurants, rest rooms, water fountains—indeed, every institution and amenity. There was even a section of town called "Nigger Town" where blacks congregated primarily on Saturdays for their shopping and socializing. There they were often exploited by white merchants who were willing to sell them many things "on time" and then reclaim them for non-payment and resale. Newspapers covered no events occurring among blacks; the only way to make the press was to commit a crime. Blacks were expected to defer to whites always and to be subservient in every situation. The rules of protocol required their approaching white residences at the back door only, being confined to theater balconies, and, of course, sitting at the back of the bus.

𝒩

Though my mother and Rosa were together constantly in their mistress-maid relationship, my mother found it very difficult ever to face the harsh realities of Rosa's day-to-day life. Rosa arrived at our basement door at the crack of dawn seven days a week, put on her apron and cap before coming upstairs, and then prepared breakfast and helped me get off to school.

Did anyone ever wonder how Rosa's own children managed or what they ate in the morning or who saw them off to school? Obviously, they were left to fend for themselves. We think of women working outside the home as a recent phenomenon of the women's movement, but black women of the South have always worked outside their homes. They have demonstrated herculean strength in rearing their own families by remote control and eking out an existence on next to nothing.

Mother and Rosa worked side by side, cleaning, cooking, and preparing to entertain. They seldom seemed happier than when they were whipping up a cake together or negotiating the purchase of fresh vegetables brought to our back door by black vendors from the rural area who would go from house to house in white neighborhoods with their horse-drawn wagons weighted down with produce. Devoted to each other, Mother and Rosa were nonetheless ever aware of what was appropriate to their racial status.

Yet, when Rosa's children were ill, my mother saw to it that they received medical attention. Leftover food was always sent home with her, and my mother and she were close enough to the same size that Rosa could wear her hand-me-downs. But when Rosa's house burned to the ground, Mother found herself unable to locate a fit dwelling within walking distance. Reluctantly, she watched Rosa crowd her growing family into a "rabbit gum house" (three rooms opening up to each other without a hallway, a rectangular box-like structure that was the standard dwelling for Negroes all over Dixie).

The house had an outside well and an outdoor toilet. The wind whistled through visible cracks in the side boarding. This

living situation troubled my parents' conscience until late in life
when at last they succeeded in securing for Rosa a small, new
house built by public funds for low-income families. Rosa was
elated at the prospect of spending her final years there, but she
has faced recurring crises trying to make payments and meet
enormous bills for electric heat. Mother and Rosa sustained each
other for a lifetime with a love and loyalty that transcended the
sick system that imprisoned them both. Countee Cullen's poem
reflects the mindset of many southern ladies I knew in Greenwood, my own mother included:

> She even thinks that up in heaven
> Her class lies late and snores,
> While poor black cherubs rise at seven
> To do celestial chores.[1]

I have not mentioned Rosa's husband, Sydney, for he
touched my life peripherally. Theirs was a common-law relationship before my parents eventually encouraged Rosa to formalize
it with marriage. Sydney was employed as the handyman at a
local florist shop where his work was erratic due to his recurring
drinking problem. My folks saw him as a loser and were put out
with him for not being more responsible. Today my sympathy is
all with Sydney. How any Negro managed to maintain a sense
of self-respect, much less sobriety, in a segregated southern town
is beyond my comprehension. Black men were figuratively—and
sometimes literally—emasculated by the system. They were deprived of both hope and dignity. They fathered children who had
a limited future. Sydney was a tragic figure, blamed for moral
failure by an immoral society that refused to see its complicity
in his dissolution.

The black man I remember with most pleasant associations
is Clifford, the hired help employed by Granddaddy to work
around the place after Uncle Henry became infirm. Clifford was
an upbeat fellow who took an interest in me and welcomed a
little boy tagging along behind him while he went about his
chores. He was enterprising and provided extra food for his table
by placing rabbit traps in nearby woods. Occasionally he invited
me to make the rounds of his traps, and we tromped through the
brush together.

How happy I was the day he agreed to give me a trap of my
very own! I took it home as a prized possession, and with the help
of my Dad, placed it behind our garage. Then, every morning, as
soon as I got out of bed, I raced out of the house to see if I had

caught a rabbit. This ritual went on for many weeks with nothing to show for my diminishing excitement. Until at last it happened: a rabbit was in my trap! Shouting to the top of my voice, I ran to the back door. "I have a rabbit! A rabbit is in my trap!" Not until years later when I was an adult did my parents confess they had conspired with Clifford to put that rabbit there; they could no longer endure my daily disappointment.

Then there was Willie. He was the house boy of a neighboring couple who worked away from home. Willie cooked and cleaned and stayed with their child when he came home from school. Their yard became the favorite place for all children in the area to play, and I was frequently among them, thus also entrusted to Willie's care. But Willie's care proved less than trustworthy, for it was he who initiated me to the mystery of sex. He would call me aside and talk about it, show me pictures of naked people and then touch me intimately. Simultaneously fascinated and frightened, I told no one. I did not know how to talk about it or to whom, certainly not to my parents.

Sex was seldom discussed openly, but everyone understood that when people talked about the danger of mixing the races, they feared interracial sex. Black men were credited with being exceptionally virile and oversexed. One of the stated purposes of segregation was "to protect southern womanhood." White men assumed that every black male would like nothing better than to bed down with a white woman. Sometimes this fear was expressed with such exaggerated emotion that it implied that white women might be willing to comply were it not for these protective barriers. Whereas, in truth, whatever miscegenation occurred was usually accounted for by white men taking advantage of black servants.

On the surface southern culture could be characterized as polite, pleasant, and peaceful. Good manners, social graces, and southern hospitality were the preferred images of the region, yet there has always been a dark side with the potential for violence lurking just beneath the veneer of societal protocol.

Surprisingly, I saw no such violence in my childhood. My parents never told me about lynchings. Not until I left home did I ever hear about a major race riot that alarmed Greenwood before my birth. I have also since learned that at the turn of the century there was a general terrorization of Negroes in the county by the so-called white caps in an attempt to get them to emigrate so whites could secure at low rent the land cultivated by black tenants. Though I now am well-informed about the intimidations and fear fostered by the Ku Klux Klan, I was not even aware of its existence when I was young. Indeed, I have never witnessed a KKK parade or seen a hooded member to this day! Somehow I was protected from this ugly underside of southern gentility. I find it impossible to reconcile the reality of such horrors with the "kind and gentle people who live in my home town."

Ironically, if there was ever any talk of problems in regard to race it was invariably referred to as "the Negro problem," never "the white problem." Blacks who complied willingly to remain in their place within the mores of segregation were called "colored people"; whereas, those judged to be troublemakers were distastefully referred to as "niggers." I realize now that my memory of a placid childhood conceals much of southern life and that there could never be any justification whatsoever for considering the system to be to any degree humane.

Be that as it may, southern culture nonetheless shaped my life, and I am a product of that segregated society. As such, I tend to shy away from controversy, for my parents taught me early that it is not polite to argue about anything or to dispute anything in public. I learned to avoid rudeness by declaring such topics as politics off-limits or to simply smile and endeavor to change the subject should a conversation seem to be getting out of hand.

My favorite foods are still soul foods. There is nothing better to eat than collard greens, black-eyed peas, and boiled okra (even though my grandfather drew the line on the latter, protesting, "I never put anything in my mouth that I don't have absolute control over.") Every Sunday morning Granddaddy served pig feet fried in batter for breakfast, a special treat for a special day, but one I no longer crave. I do, however, fit the stereotype of the southern preacher in my inordinate love for fried chicken.

My speech was also heavily acculturated despite my being drilled in elocution as a boy and competing in oratorical contests when a teen. At divinity school my speech professor kindly sensitized me to the strange way I pronounced certain words, such as saying "shadder" for "shadow." One of the few ways whites and blacks freely intermingled was in a shared southern drawl.

High school days were the happiest time of my growing-up years. I attended a large consolidated school that brought to-

gether the offspring of blue-collar mill folk and the children of
the privileged. Blacks, of course, had a makeshift school of their
own from which most dropped out long before graduation. Even
so, high school did teach me democratic ideals. The politics of
student government gave me early experience in skills put to
more serious use in later years. My high school yearbook predicted, "Bob will be either a preacher or a politician," vocations
I have since discovered are at times virtually synonymous. The
motto of our principal stays with me: "Do right because it is right
and not because you are afraid to do wrong." On weekends
during those years I worked at Belk's Department Store where
black farm and factory laborers purchased their overalls and
work clothes. It was there that I discovered how much I enjoyed
relating to different types of people.

It saddens me to acknowledge that through all of this, from
my earliest formative years until I finished public school, there
was not a single person who called into question the morality of
the segregated society that surrounded me. Everyone assumed
that the South had found the ideal solution for blacks and whites
to live in proximity yet completely apart. No one anticipated this
would ever change.

Even the church, that institution which remains at the center of southern life and which influenced me more than any
other, made peace with segregation. Never once during all my
growing-up years did it cause me to see any inconsistency in the
racial practices of the community with Christianity. I turn now
to consider the role of the church in sanctioning that status quo.

Chapter 3

"South of God"

Upon meeting a new acquaintance in the South, you are likely to be asked early in the conversation, "What church do you go to?" Southerners simply assume that everyone belongs to a church and that it is at the center of their lives. This was more the case in my youth than it is today, for secular erosion is occurring below the Mason-Dixon line just like everywhere else, though at a much slower pace.

Baptists are still by far the largest church group in Greenwood, with Methodists not far behind. The old joke says that when Baptists become educated, they become Presbytcrians; when they get rich, they become Episcopalians. But whatever the denominational label, all religious bodies "South of God" seem to be cut from the same cloth and, for a long time, they all put up a united front to perpetuate segregation. This is not surprising since nearly every major Protestant group split North and South about the time of the Civil War. Despite any current rationalization to the contrary, the racial issue accounted for the division. The precise controversy that precipitated the break of the Southern Baptist Convention from the national body was whether missionaries could be permitted to own slaves. Following the war, Negroes abandoned the balconies of their masters' congregation and established congregations of their own, sometimes founding an alternate First Baptist Church close by the one they had left. To this day in Raleigh, there are two First Baptist Churches that stand on opposite corners of Capitol Square.

The First Baptist Church of Greenwood was the only church I knew until I went away to college. Then I discovered that my home church was by no means typical of our predominantly rural denomination. Whereas many Baptists were loudly fundamentalist, First Baptist would best be described as a conservative congregation without a strident tone of voice and where everything was done decently and in order.

As the establishment congregation of the Baptist conglomerate, members regarded themselves as the respectable people of the town. Most folk were fairly well educated and had sufficient money to live a comfortable life. They wanted to be comfortable in their religion, too. In later years this church became known as a "liberal" church, which in South Carolina was not meant to suggest social gospel but rather that the service of worship was more liturgical, that it had a divided chancel, and that the people no longer called the worship space an "auditorium" but a sanctuary. Today it also means that dances are sponsored by the church for its young people and that it tolerates occasional cocktails for deacons, even in one another's company.

As I look back upon my religious upbringing, I see no indication of racial barriers having been any weaker in the church than anywhere else in southern life. The indictment by the Swedish sociologist, Gunnar Myrdal, in his monumental study of racial relationships in the United States, *An American Dilemma*, published in 1944, coincides with my experience:

> Viewed as an instrument of collective action to improve the Negro's position in American society, the church has been relatively inefficient and uninfluential. In the South it has not taken a lead in attacking the caste system or even in bringing about minor reforms . . . this might be deemed deplorable, but it should not be surprising. Christian churches generally have, for the most part, conformed to the power situation of time and locality.[1]

It is a harsh judgment, but the truth of it cannot be questioned.

Nonetheless, something happened to me in that nurturing community of faith that led to my own eventual role in the racial revolution. Though at the time I was a victim of the same mindset as everyone else, the saturation with Scripture served me well when at last I realized that if "God is no respecter of persons," this surely means the Negro person as well as the white person. I became biblically literate as I listened to a corps of faithful

Sunday school teachers and countless exegetical sermons. Like explosives with delayed timing devices, the biblical message eventually jolted my life and made it imperative for me to challenge the culture that had cradled me. Gradually I realized that what I heard in church and what I saw in the world around me were glaring in their inconsistency.

I have many wonderful and warm memories of First Baptist Church. Whenever the doors were open, our family was always there. We sat in the same place at every service: the first pew down front with my grandfather sitting on the aisle and all his children, in-laws, and grandchildren there beside him. I remember counting organ pipes while the preacher preached and going home after the service to mock and mimic the shrill soprano soloist, much to the amusement of my parents. Before the present new Gothic sanctuary was built, the "auditorium" was a spacious facility with overflow areas for annual revivals. A musty smell pervaded the place, and on hot, humid, summer Sundays we kept the sweat to a minimum by cooling ourselves with "courtesy of the funeral home" fans. (Maybe this accounts for the southern phrase "I'm so hot I could die!") I remember building bird houses at Vacation Bible School (I never understood why), and I recall everyone wearing a rose on Mother's Day, a red one if she were alive and a white one if deceased.

I went to church for four regular events every Sunday: Sunday school, "preaching," B.Y.P.U. (Baptist Young Peoples' Union), and the evening service. We were also there on Wednesdays for very informal prayer meetings. The preacher would drone on for what seemed like forever in a never-ending series about the meaning of *Pilgrim's Progress*. He would call on different persons to pray, including some of the young people. Since my father and I had the same name, when the pastor requested Robert Seymour to lead in prayer, my dad would sometimes nudge me and insist, "He means you, Son." The same familiar petitions were offered up week after week although Baptists were on record as being against set prayers.

Blacks were never a part of anything that happened at our church. The only exception would be an occasional funeral when a family servant would be invited to sit with the mourners of the household where she worked. Of course, there was a Negro janitor, self-effacing and never visible to the worshiping congregation even though he might be in the building. A large signboard on the church lawn announced sermon titles to passers-by, and, ironically, beneath it appeared an open invitation:

"Everyone Welcome." Both blacks and whites knew how to translate the message; it really meant "whites only."

Scripture warns against "trumpets of uncertain sound." There was no uncertainty in the message at First Baptist. Everyone clearly understood that Christianity was compatible with segregation. The status quo was deemed acceptable to God, and the church bestowed its blessing. There was an unspoken agreement among all parties. No one would challenge the system; no one would rock the boat, most especially the preacher.

People believed that segregation was God's intended order of creation. Some churches taught that Negroes were the descendants of Noah's son, Ham, and were the recipients of the curse to become "hewers of wood and drawers of water" (Joshua 9:23). I do not recall being taught this at First Baptist, but teachers did point out repeatedly that just as various species of birds do not mix but remain separate from other species, so God did not intend members of the black and white races to intermingle.

James McBride Dabbs, a former president of the Southern Regional Council (which is one of the South's oldest and most effective organizations committed to improving the plight of Negroes), used to say that the fact that southern Christians felt the need to justify segregation was in itself a tribute to the Christian tradition. The Greeks and the Romans didn't justify slavery; they didn't have to. But obviously, Christian principles presented a conflict with the concept of segregation; therefore, its proponents were obligated to create a defense. He also noted that most Christians tend to become rather shrill when they try to make a case for it.

Another common argument offered to bolster the separation was that segregation had nothing to do with racial prejudice but represented racial preference. "We know our colored people, and this is the way they want it," southerners assured, never seeing that the apparent consent of blacks to such statements might be related to their fear of reprisal should they ever challenge it. All whites agreed that prejudice was wrong but racial preference was acceptable, indeed, desirable, for it would be freely chosen. When the leading Baptist pastor in Texas, W.A. Criswell, spoke to the South Carolina legislature at the beginning of the civil rights movement and said, "Anyone who believes in integration is dead from the neck up," he spoke for the large rank and file of fellow worshipers of whatever their denomination all over the South. Whites insisted, "Negroes prefer segregation." No one ever confessed, "We imposed it."

This logic was more easily implemented among Baptists because of their theological understanding of what constitutes a church. "We have *our* churches, and they have *their* churches," people said. The doctrine of the one universal church that belongs to God and to which all belong had few proponents, for it would have threatened the mentality of separateness. A great many Baptists frequently speak of churches rather than of *the* church. Instead of one body of believers, they understand church as multiple congregations, each autonomous and responsible for governing its own affairs. Thus, there is no ecclesiastical hierarchy to promulgate orthodoxy in either theology or ethics. Such loose associations tend to make congeniality a primary consideration for joining a particular congregation. The church is vulnerable to taking on the characteristics of a social club where "your friends are my friends, and my friends are your friends; the more we get together, the happier we'll be."

This perception prepared the way not only for racial separation but for choosing one's church according to one's class. In every southern town the First Baptist Church was usually the most prestigious, attracting primarily professional people, whereas other Baptist congregations were composed largely of blue-collar folk. In our textile town, each mill village had a separate congregation. Not infrequently, the mill management made generous financial contributions and even in some cases paid the preacher's salary. Why would they do this? It was to insure that the focus of the pulpit would be on spiritual matters and to discourage any consideration of worker grievances or, God forbid, a labor union.

Textile magnate J.C. Self had never made a profession of faith; he did not belong to a church nor attend one, which was surprising for a prominent leader in the South. This was a matter of some concern among community church leaders, for they judged Self not only to be a solid citizen but also a good man whose lifestyle was in step with the faithful. On one occasion, after completing the construction of an entire new village with attractive brick houses for all his mill "hands," Self let it be known that he wanted to build a new church for the people who lived there and that he would do it in memory of his mother. Everyone applauded this generous offer, including my grandfather who admired Mr. Self and was flattered whenever Self sought him out as a friend. When the Callie Self Memorial Baptist Church was almost finished (complete with a carillon bell tower purchased from the New York World's Fair), Self contacted my grandfather to ask if he could suggest an outstanding Baptist preacher to come for the dedication service. Grandaddy knew just the man: Dr. George W. Truett, an outstanding pulpiteer produced by Southern Baptists. He was a gentleman who was widely admired for his scholarship, statesmanship, and persuasive ability.

I will never forget that service. Apparently my grandfather had alerted Truett to Self's unsaved condition, and the famous preacher agreed to come for the primary purpose of persuading Self to make a public decision for the Lord. Our family had tickets (so great was the expected crowd), and we all sat on the second pew, right behind the Self family. The gist of the sermon was this: you can give God many things, but what God really wants most of all is self. "God wants *self!*" Truett thundered repeatedly, punning the name of his host so pointedly that not only was Mr. Self squirming, we all were—but to no avail. Self refused to be moved. He remained outside the organized church for the balance of his life.

This incident illustrates the primary thrust of southern preaching. To win such a man today might be seen as a great victory for social justice since it would influence his use of wealth and industry, but back then, the primary concern was for a person's eternal salvation. Personal soul winning is still the principal agenda of the southern church. People are lured out of the world and brought into the church, but rarely are they challenged to go back into the world to change it. They are given the impression that the work of the church is not the work of the world but, rather, being involved in church-related activities, shoring up the institution, and going out to win other unchurched folk to bring them in.

The idea of the church as God's instrument for radically reordering the society around it was seldom grasped. Most pulpit fare aimed at personal transformation and included sermons heavy with theological doctrine. More attention was given to preparing people for the next life than for making over this one. Southerners could only be thankful for such preaching, for subconsciously all surely realized they simply could not afford to scrutinize their Jim Crow culture in the light of the gospel of Jesus.

Sadly, the social gospel did not touch the South significantly until after the civil rights movement was history. The only so-called social issue consistently addressed by Baptists was alcoholism. Once each quarter both young people and adults had a temperance lesson in Sunday school. I grew up thinking that taking a drink was the ultimate evil. Southern churches preached against personal iniquities, not social injustices. How ironic that the pioneer of Christian social ethics, Walter Rauschenbusch, was a Baptist, yet his persuasive thought about establishing the kingdom of God never penetrated southern religion. Naively, the southern church assumed that if you evangelize enough people to Christ, all social evils would eventually disappear. It would not be necessary to address them directly. Yet despite nonstop revivalism and ever-increasing numbers of the converted, segregation remained rigidly in place, never budging.

The role of the church in the southern United States and Soviet Russia at this time was remarkably similar. In Russia, the functions of the church were limited by the communist government to worship, piety, and prayer—nothing more. No prophetic ministry was permitted, no expression of concern about social issues, no emphasis on the Christian implications of political policies; yet many American laypeople wanted their churches here to be just as silent and irrelevant as there.

Even so, church folk extolled the virtues of compassion and charity; kindness to individuals in need could be offered to anybody, whether black or white. Segregationists learned how to accommodate expressions of mercy within the system and never felt threatened by them. Beneficent whites were often generous in coming to the rescue of blacks in their times of personal crisis with the full assurance that it was their Christian duty to do so, yet with the understanding that this never need entail any social association. All understood their places as many a "Lady Bountiful" ameliorated some of the harsher deprivations suffered by Negroes. My mother was a classic example. She would move heaven and earth to help Rosa in any time of crisis, as was the case when Rosa's son, Calvin, was born with an abnormal heart condition and needed the medical attention of a specialist.

Consistently, whites would say, "We love our colored people," and in a condescending, paternalistic way, indeed they did. There is no doubt of my mother's love for Rosa, though clearly the love was compromised. Perhaps the best analogy to account for the affection voiced by whites and often reciprocated by blacks is that of the relationship of parent to child. Just as a parent feels a child is not ready to be given full freedom and responsibility since the child cannot yet know what is best, so whites rationalized that Negroes needed to be kept within certain limits for their own well-being. A part of the resentment that

surfaced later as the civil rights movement gained momentum
was bewilderment on the part of the whites over the child no
longer wanting to be treated like one.

Southerners heard countless sermons on the parable of the
good Samaritan that emphasized that final phrase, "Go, and do
thou likewise." They understood that the Negro was indeed their
neighbor, but obviously, it did not cocur to many that the man
was in the ditch because of a governmental system that failed to
prevent such tragedies in the first place. A more relevant sermon
might have admonished, "Clean up the Jericho Roads!"

The Old South never understood that love is no substitute for
justice. Whites deprived blacks of their political rights because
they judged themselves more capable of doing the governing.
Whites were puzzled by Negroes becoming so demanding since
they were so self-assured about having the Negroes best interests
at heart. They were slow to learn the audacity of depriving people of basic elementary rights. They failed to grasp the truth that
love can never be less than justice and that anything claiming to
be love at the expense of justice is at best a diseased love.

Even mission work suffered from this less-than-complete
love. Through the Southern Baptist emphasis on world missions,
appeal for support of foreign missionaries was unrelenting.
Ironically, Africa generated more sustained interest than any
other continent. A hierarchy of organizational structures to
guarantee missionary education for every age group included
Sunbeams for young children, Royal Ambassadors and Girls
Auxiliary for teens, and the Woman's Missionary Society and
Brotherhood for adults. Everyone perceived mission work as
something that took place elsewhere in the world. Mission support was primarily a matter of raising money to send overseas.
Although members were aware of home mission endeavors in
other areas of the United States, no one ever felt that local problems on their own home front would qualify as a mission field,
for "we have no problems here."

The discrepancy between what was preached afar and what
was practiced at home created very awkward situations when
missionaries began to send African nationals to this country for
their college education. When these students arrived on southern campuses, church people tried to resolve the dilemma by
adopting a double standard and offering foreign students facilities and courtesies denied local blacks. This confused the for-

eigners and angered Negroes who could not appreciate the difference between American blacks and African blacks. Thus, the agenda for saving the souls of the world's colored peoples boomeranged when these souls appeared in human flesh and expected to be accepted fully into the Christian fellowship. This problem of welcoming black students from overseas created more of a crisis in the church than in any other place. The possibility of a black person attending a worship service in a white church traumatized people, causing the Africans to sense the alienation and conflicting emotions. The intensity of the feelings proved so threatening that many of these young people from abroad quietly withdrew and ended up becoming a part of the local black congregations instead of the white churches that took credit for their conversion to Christianity. The situation was embarrassing to the extreme, for it was never more clear than when a choice had to be made between one's religious faith and segregation, that segregation would remain intact and Christianity would be compromised. As late as 1966, the pastor of the Tatnall Square Baptist Church, located on the campus of Mercer University in Macon, Georgia, was forcibly terminated for admitting a black college student from Ghana into the congregation.

Most whites had little exposure to black churches. Whereas Sunday was indeed a day of rest for white Christians, it was never that for many Negroes. Rosa was expected to prepare a huge dinner every Sunday, and anticipation of it made many a boring sermon more bearable for me. The remainder of the day was for leisure or visiting with relatives until time to return to church for evening activities. I recall little concern expressed for Rosa and her family regarding their church attendance. Either she seldom went or services were available to her at other times.

A favorite sport for teens on Sunday nights after worship was to cruise through the unpaved streets of the "nigger section" and bait people standing beside the road with prejudicial slurs or to drive slowly by their churches and laugh as we listened to loud singing and shouting, unlike anything we ever heard in our own sedate congregations.

Accustomed to the irrelevance of much that was said in their own churches, white Christians never dreamed that the black church could become a seedbed for revolution. Yet this was the only institution where blacks were free of white domination and that they could claim as their own. Though much of the preaching promised a better life in the hereafter, just as in the white church, their church was also a place where persons could un-

burden themselves to one another about the cruelty and injustices suffered in their day-to-day lives. It is not surprising that the
civil rights movement took root in the black church and that it
became the primary base of support for protests against segregation all over the South.

❧

Concurrent with my growing up years, but unknown to me
at the time, was a trumpet of more certain sound being faintly
heard across the South. It was made by a small group of black
and white Christians who banded together and called themselves
the Fellowship of Southern Churchmen. They published a provocative journal, *Prophetic Religion*, and though the voice of this
organization attracted little attention, it was nonetheless an
early warning signal to southerners who were committed to
perpetuating segregation forever.

The Fellowship exposed the unconscionable gap between
the church's profession of faith and its day-by-day practice. The
Fellowship believed that the church was meant to be used by God
for creating a new earth. It announced a New Reformation and
appealed for new leadership. The courageous summons to action
amounted to little more than a voice crying in the wilderness, yet
it was a significant crack in the wall. The southern church, still
bound hand and foot in the strait jacket of segregation, could not
yet imagine a new social order that would be open to all.

Chapter 4

Cracks in the Wall

Recent history verified the prophetic judgment of sociologist Gunnar Myrdal that the church would not likely change until the community around it had changed. Up until the Second World War, southern churches, both black and white, generally conformed to the power structure of their time and locality, but the uprooting and dislocation of so many people of both races during those years of national emergency permanently altered southern society with no hope of its ever returning to its prewar provincialism.

My college years coincided with this turbulent period. Plans for my education and career moved in totally unexpected directions. Normally I would have followed the safe route prescribed for any South Carolina Baptist youth interested in professional ministry by attending Furman University and Southern Seminary, but once I turned my life over to the Navy, all decisions about where I would study were no longer mine. As a result, I acquired a strange set of academic credentials. I became a Baptist preacher who was never a student in a Baptist school.

Becoming a preacher was a vocational choice that seemed in place from my earliest days; I never considered anything else. The church had been at the center of my life during all my formative years. I had been surrounded by preachers to whom hospitality had been extended frequently in both my grandfather's and parents' homes, and I am sure the esteem they had in my family influenced my decision. I cannot pinpoint any Damascus Road experience; I simply grew up with the certainty that this was what I was meant to do with my life.

As a teenager, this predisposition was reinforced by revivalist persuasion. On several occasions, especially at summer assemblies at the Southern Baptist grounds in Ridgecrest, North Carolina, I felt prompted to go forward in response to the evangelist's invitation to declare my intention "to go into full-time Christian service." In retrospect, I wonder if the use of this phrase in reference to a church-related vocation might also have influenced my career direction, for it seemed to imply that church employment options were on a higher level in the eyes of God than any others. Later I challenged this concept when I realized that any worthwhile work for the well-being of God's world would surely be equally acceptable in God's sight.

At the outset, my understanding of what a clergyman did was a reflection of the narrow, traditional role modeling of my upbringing. I had no awareness then of the social component of the gospel, nor had I experienced any prophetic call to turn the world upside down. I thought that the preacher's primary task was to fish people out of life's turbulent sea and then put them into that ecclesiastical marineland called the church where they would be kept safe and secure until Judgment Day. I sensed no conflict between discipleship and citizenship, nor had I been given any vision of the faith community as a divine agent for social change. Indeed, such enlightened understandings did not significantly penetrate my southern mindset until after I had completed my undergraduate college education! This makes me suspect that my professors may have been as blind to the gravity of the racial situation as I was or that they were intimidated into playing the tune for which the pipers were paid.

In one sense the war served the nation well by making it impossible for southerners to maintain their isolation. It forced a reevaluation of insular ideas. In the mid-forties everything was in a state of flux. Military orders mandated extensive travel and exposed people to places very different from the familiarity of home. A friend stationed in New York City welcomed his missionary-minded mother for a visit. Noting her acute discomfort as she found herself squeezed between two black men on a crowded subway, her son chided, "Mother, you can send it to them, but it sure is hard for you to take it to them."

Train travel began to give way to planes, and the radio was

about to be replaced by television. Rapid movement and immediate communication enabled persons everywhere to become
better informed about one other. Southern blacks heard about
a wider world "up North" where better opportunities beckoned
and where the indignity of discrimination was less overtly apparent. Every night when the Silver Meteor stopped in Greenwood,
there were large numbers of Negroes on the platform, apprehen-
sively making an exodus to a strange new world. They must have
felt like the character Noah in an old black folk play when he
said, "Seems like everything nailed down is comin' loose!" What
a painfully wrenching experience it must have have been for
these poor blacks to leave their loved ones to face the insecurity
of the unknown, wondering if they would ever return to the
South.

In Dixie, white and black train passengers were assigned to
separate cars, but the war years took many southerners beyond
their provincial borders. Some surely experienced what Jan
Struther describes in these lines:

> Nine hours late: and even that ill-matched couple
> On the front seat—the lady with the blue-white hair
> And the young Negro soldier, silent and supple—
> Who, at the journey's start,
> Sat ramrod straight, aware of one another
> Beyond invisible bars, sister and brother
> Both ill at ease, yet both without escape
> From a base-born, base-bred,
> Nebulous, opposite yet identical dread
> (He of a white folks' glance he's learned to fear,
> She of a touch she feels is kin to rape)
> Even these two now sleep: they're drowned in peace,
> White head and black head nodding an inch apart.
> Exhaustion brings oblivion, lulls mistrust,
> Falls blindly on the just and the unjust,
> Quenches discrimination, gives release
> From self-forged barriers to the human heart.[1]

Travel for blacks through the South was seldom without
fear. Few whites ever considered the difficulties and inconve-
niences imposed upon blacks who risked trips by car on southern highways. There were no public facilities available anywhere for food or overnight lodging except in segregated
sections of cities. Blacks had to plot their itinerary from one
friend's house to another or journey long distances without rest.

Many white restaurants would serve meals out of a back door
but seldom had places for black customers to eat on the premises. Blacks could buy gas anywhere but were prohibited from
using the "white only" restrooms. Forced to relieve themselves
in wooded areas beside the road, they were then liable to being
arrested for exposing themselves in public. Furthermore, there
was always the constant danger of being stopped by a white
policeman on some trumped-up charge and having no recourse
but to pay dearly for the alleged infraction of the law, whether
guilty or innocent. Maids sometimes traveled with the families
for whom they worked to be baby-sitters and cooks at the beach
cottage or the mountain cabin. Rosa's first journey to the coast
was with my parents who planned a special trip to show her the
ocean.

My first venture living away from home still kept me within
the secure confines of South Carolina. When I learned it was
possible to delay entering the Armed Service until after my freshman year of college, my father thought it would be to my advantage to spend it at the Citadel, the state military institution in
Charleston from which he had graduated. He was convinced that
every growing boy should have such disciplined training "to
teach him how to hang up his clothes after he takes them off."
(My wife complains that I never learned.)

I was miserable there. Upperclasssmen victimized freshmen
from dawn until dark with approved hazing, which permitted
them to make constant and often unreasonable demands and to
heap merciless humiliations upon them at every turn. I can still
hear the captain of our company unit snarling and shouting at
full volume, "You putrid pieces of protoplasm!" All such abuses
were intended, of course, to make men of us, as was also the rigid
schedule, the petty rules, and the necessity of learning how to
assemble and disassemble an M-1 rifle blindfolded! My sense of
self-esteem had seldom been so low, yet for generations many
southerners sought military training for their sons as a desirable
dimension of their education. Fortunately, many such military
prep schools, which once blanketed the region, have fallen out
of fashion and closed.

The Citadel allowed no Negroes to come on campus except
those employed in the kitchen, laundry, or on the ground crews.
Cheerleaders waved the Confederate flag at all athletic events.
No tour of historic Charleston with visitors was judged complete

without seeing the well-preserved slave market. Decades later, when federal law finally forced the admission of several blacks to the student body, they showed great courage in surviving there.

Novelist Pat Conroy chronicles an account of this in his thinly veiled fictionalized story of the Citadel, *The Lords of Discipline*. Administrators adamantly protested his accurate, sadistic image of the school and refused permission for Hollywood to film the movie version on campus. More recently, the magnificent old city revealed its ability to adjust to change by producing a celebrated rendering of Gershwin's *Porgy and Bess* in its intended Charleston setting. The fete brought blacks and whites together socially to claim with delayed pride their shared heritage.

Before my freshman year at the Citadel had barely begun, I had to reckon with the draft board, which made me understand that I would be in uniform soon. The possibility of becoming a conscientious objector never crossed my mind. Pacifism was not even discussed in our church, and besides, to defeat Hitler seemed like a righteous crusade. As the conflict escalated and I anticipated my place within it, I learned of a new program launched by the Navy, called V-12, that promised undergraduates an extension of their education after enlisting. I had the good fortune not only of being accepted but also of being cleared as a candidate for a prechaplaincy curriculum. This virtually guaranteed the continuation of my studies straight through seminary.

The V-12 program was an ambitious undertaking for the Navy. Preparing for the possibility of a long war, the Navy conceived the program as a way of insuring a source of well-trained officers while at the same time enabling more than 130 institutions of higher learning to sustain their student bodies until the war's end. For the first time in the nation's history, the president directed that the educational program be open to anyone, irrespective of race. In fact, some Negroes were included and advanced to high places of leadership, though the Navy accommodated Jim Crow customs by sending no Negroes to southern campuses.

Imagine the incredulous response of my parents when my Navy orders arrived and I was notified to report to Newberry College, a small Lutheran school less than forty miles from home! They were jubilant, but I was less than happy at the prospect of being deprived of expected travel. For the equivalent of two academic years, I flourished in the hospitable environment of small-town America, and my poor mother entertained a contingent of sailors every weekend as house guests. Many Navymates came from the North or Midwest and had little appreciation for Rosa's grits at breakfast, but I quickly discovered that the racial attitudes prevalent in the South were widely shared by the nation as a whole. Convincing evidence of this conclusion was a much appreciated minstrel show produced by Navy trainees in which southerners and Yankees alike blackened their faces together and entertained the base at the cost of further entrenching prejudice against colored people. Even the Navy commandant commended the cast profusely for putting together such an amusing program.

Being more interested in Duke University's academic program, I requested and received permission to transfer. The Gothic quadrangle seemed more like a military fortress than a college, for units of the Army, Navy, and Air Force occupied most of the campus. Students in uniform were everywhere. Academics were far more demanding there and left little time for anything else. However, like Newberry, Duke was an all-white institution. Blacks were not welcome on campus except in traditional servant roles, and it was rumored that administrative rules prohibited any campus group from inviting any black, however famous nationally, to speak on the premises. There was no resistance to this racist climate, not even from the divinity school. A great university was thus locked in southern mores, and its Methodist roots made no difference in ameliorating the condition.

After I left home for college, my contacts with Rosa were less frequent. Since she was illiterate, she could not communicate by mail, and in my student days no one called long distance except in emergencies. Later, during my professional career, Rosa discovered greeting cards as a way of keeping in touch. Although she could not write, she did learn how to inscribe her signature. On my birthday, at Christmas and Easter and other special occasions, I would hear from her. She afforded a strong link to the Old South that never let me go.

✿

Not until I was twenty years old did I live outside the South and see blacks and whites living together as equals for the first time. Yale Divinity School in Connecticut was the place where the Navy trained its chaplains. After a summer detour to boot camp, I arrived in New Haven as a midshipman to begin three of my happiest years in a setting that quickly changed my life irrevocably.

There were fewer than ten Negroes in the student body, but two of them resided near me in the same dormitory. They never knew what an enormous influence they exerted over me as we slept under the same roof and shaved before the same mirrors morning after morning, side by side. My previous associations with blacks had always been with persons of limited education who were confined to menial employment, like Clifford, Sydney, and Rosa. When I then found myself in the presence of black people who were my peers, the impact can only be compared to something akin to a religious conversion. Persuasive arguments about racial equality can never be as effective as the existential experience of being placed in the company of equals.

The situation at Yale seemed even more strange because the domestic servants who cleaned and cooked were all white. Suddenly, the world seemed topsy-turvy as I watched the role reversal of white people waiting on black people! Though I had anticipated the possibility of finding myself in a setting where southern customs did not apply, I was unprepared for emotions that insistently reminded me that these arrangements were improper.

Vestiges of prejudice lingered despite my rapid conversion to the new order. I soon had absolutely no doubt intellectually that racial inclusiveness was the way things should be. My ability to affirm the rightness of a community in which everyone was accepted as equal brought with it a sense of inward liberation. This conviction remains at the heart of my being even though to this day my mind cannot always dictate the correct corresponding feeling. My shock upon first seeing a black woman kiss a white man reverberates within me still.

I "found myself" at Yale. In many ways it was a painful discovery, for I had to see beyond the stereotypes that people from other parts of the country had about the South and imposed on me. Southerners were judged not only to be prejudiced, but ignorant, and even uncouth. Yankees considered our speech charming and amusing, but also sloven. Some seemed surprised that South Carolinians even wore shoes. My being a Southern Baptist did not help matters, for we were perceived as a holy-roller sect. Most maddening of all, however, was the northern-

ers' habit of retaining their distorted ideas while judging me to
be an exception to the southern norm.

They forced me to see the South through their eyes. I had
to put into perspective aspects of southern culture that I had
never been willing to scrutinize before. Convincing statistics
showed that we were the stepchild of the nation. High poverty
levels and low education scores could not be debated, and no
one doubted that such shocking conditions were inseparably
related to segregation.

My exposure to new thinking regarding the racial issue was
of some concern to my parents, especially my father. He felt
personally threatened in his relationship to me as he realized on
my visits home that I no longer accepted the rationale of the
southern way of life and, further, could not keep quiet about my
unpopular views.

It pains me to recall those heated discussions that inevitably ended in acute frustration and anger. My mother tried to
temper them by a cautious willingness to concede the logic of
my position, but not so with my father. He would conclude his
case with what he considered a reasonable compromise:
"When in Rome, you must do as the Romans do!" To which I
replied with unconcealed pleasure, "Remember the Christians
in Rome who, rather than conform, chose to be fed to the
lions!" I wonder now what Rosa must have been thinking as
she overheard some of the arguments from the kitchen. Occasionally my mother would make an effort to shush the volume
lest Rosa take personally some of the judgments being made
against black people in general.

My stand against segregation also threatened First Baptist
Church whose favorite son would no doubt soon ask to be ordained there. My parents understood the congregation's ambivalence toward me but resented that I was seldom asked to supply
the pulpit. They suspected that this was due to anxiety about
what I might say regarding the racial issue.

The anxiety was well founded. I read in the *Index-Journal*,
Greenwood's daily newspaper which I received at Yale, that the
American Legion planned to erect a memorial on the town
square to honor World War II dead. I could scarcely believe it
when I read further that the names of white servicemen would
be inscribed at the top of the memorial marker and the names
of black servicemen on the bottom. Segregation in stone! It was
to be arranged in this way so that the soldiers could "get full
credit for their participation." I was outraged; how could anyone

be so stupid? How could you honor those who died to preserve democracy by a project that refused to acknowledge the equality of everyone, even in death? The monument would symbolize the defeat for Negroes in securing the very thing for which they had fought and died.

I drafted an indignant letter to the editor, but failed to alert my parents that it would appear in the local press. Mother later described what happened. She was still in bed on Sunday morning perusing the weekend edition of the *Index* when she spotted my correspondence. Daddy was in the adjacent bathroom getting ready to shower and singing his favorite gospel song, "When the Roll Is Called Up Yonder," conditioning himself for church.

"Look what's in the paper," Mother shouted.

"Who's dead?" Daddy asked.

"Worse than that," she wailed.

My poor parents were so mortified by my epistle that it almost took more courage than they could muster to face people at First Baptist that day. Mother reported that close friends comforted her while others tried to ignore the unfortunate incident, though these betrayed their awareness with a knowing look when they exchanged their customary Sunday greetings.

Despite the necessity of weathering such embarrassments, my folks were genuinely proud of my being at Yale. They could see how happy I was there and were convinced of the superiority of my educational opportunity. Should anyone question the wisdom of a Southern Baptist being in such a liberal place, my parents could always blame my being there on the Navy. When the war ended at the close of my first year, the Navy severed my relationship with no strings attached. Then, free to leave Yale and transfer elsewhere, there was not even a discussion of an alternative. I would remain in New Haven.

This was the best thing that ever happened to me. I often wonder whom I might have become had I not been sent to Yale. Before Yale Divinity School I was a conservative fundamentalist, and although academic biblical criticism shook the foundations of my faith, I emerged with a much stronger and more intelligent understanding of my religion. Now I knew that Christianity does not stand or fall by the worship of a book but that the Living God speaks even so through this less-than-perfect literature.

Theology confused me. European theologian Karl Barth was beginning to be the big name in seminaries, and neoorthodoxy attracted a large following. Never having moved out of orthodoxy into liberalism, I was baffled by the movement away from liberalism, which assumed that I had been exposed to something that had not even slightly touched my life. People seemed excited about having rediscovered the reality of sin, something that as a Southern Baptist I had never had occasion to lose. The new theological vocabulary was remarkably similar to what I had heard all my life, and it took me a long time to appreciate the differences in definitions. I feel a little deprived for having missed out on twentieth-century liberalism and am still reticent to put myself in the neoorthodox camp.

My student generation was blessed by a star-studded Yale faculty: Roland Bainton in church history, Robert Calhoun in historical theology, Richard Niebuhr in Christian ethics, Halford Luccock in preaching, and Liston Pope in social ethics. It was a heady atmosphere, for the students were also top caliber from across the nation. These were the brightest and the best. Being a part of this stimulating community of scholars and learners enhanced my self-esteem immeasurably. Whereas, as an undergraduate, I sometimes felt a little apologetic in identifying myself as a ministerial student because "pre-theologs" seemed a rather mediocre bunch, at Yale I felt proud for the privilege of being numbered among such a distinguished group.

I learned there the meaning of the word "ecumenical," not simply as a concept but as a reality. The large word in our life together was *Christian*, seldom our respective denominational labels. Nearly every major Protestant group was represented, as well as several pioneering Roman Catholics. A few women were also on the scene but were not yet protesting the sexism of the church. Worship and prayer strengthened our relationships as we shared from our various liturgical traditions. Each morning students from Bushnell House residence stopped by the prayer chapel for a time of silence before breakfast. One friend never made it even once during the entire three years, though he could sometimes be heard shouting from his window as we left him behind, "You guys, who worship God at this ungodly hour and expect God to be there!"

Richard Niebuhr's *Christ and Culture* gave me valuable insight about the ways the church has related to culture through the centuries. When he lectured about societies in which the church and culture were assumed to be one and the same, I knew he was describing the American South. I was energized by the hope that someday the southern church might emulate an alternate style and see itself as *against* culture and seek to transform it.

Social ethics showed the way, and Liston Pope awakened me to the social gospel. It all seems so obvious now, that loving God with heart, mind, and soul is inseparably related to loving one's neighbor as oneself. These are not two commandments; they are one. Personal gospel and social gospel go hand in hand. Not until Yale did the full impact of this insight begin to inspire the direction of my life and become the mainspring of my later ministry in the South.

Pope took our ethics class on a field trip to New York City where we feasted in Harlem at one of Father Divine's Heavenly Kitchens. Sumptuous meals of southern soul food, just like Rosa's, were served by angels "miraculously" and without cost to all who came. Despite the unorthodox theology, it was an impressive evidence of a caring and genuine community among the disenfranchised.

Social activists from the divinity school picketed the film *Song of the South,* because the stories of Joel Chandler Harris were judged prejudicial in their stereotypes of blacks. I refused to participate for I felt the film depicted a unique part of southern culture that need not be sacrificed, just as Negro spirituals remain a prized part of our musical heritage.

We joked about pulpiteers who preached only the comforting reassuring words of a personal gospel. We asked, "Do you know the difference between the apostle Paul and Norman Vincent Peale?" The answer: "Paul is appealing and Peale is appalling." Luccock taught that balanced preaching was always twofold in its purpose: "To comfort the afflicted and to afflict the comfortable."

There were repeated reminders of home. Dean Luther Weigle was chairman of the committee that was translating the Revised Standard Version of Scripture. I met him in the hall one day and he asked, "Aren't you from South Carolina, Bob? Have you ever heard of a little town named Due West?"

"Yes," I acknowledged, "it is near Greenwood."

"Well," he replied, "I received a can of ashes from there in the mail today. They had a Bible burning to protest our changing the word 'virgin' in Isaiah and translating it 'young woman' instead."

This was the kind of "heresy" southerners would expect from a place like Yale Divinity School.

The senior chapel address by a classmate from the South

spoke for many of us in a masterful meditation on the story of
Peter in the courtyard, where he was "following Jesus afar off"
and was "betrayed by an accent." Despite classes in speech and
preaching, my southern accent was still there, and with it, a
stigma. Although there were opportunities for me to remain in
the North, I knew I could never feel comfortable outside the
South and determined to return. I sensed something momentous
was about to occur there, and I wanted to be a part of it.

Not until graduation did I lure my dad to Yale. I hosted a
social event for seminary faculty and friends to meet my parents
and included the black students who lived in my residence hall.
I was apprehensive about how my father would respond to the
situation, but he came through with flying colors. He not only
welcomed the Negroes; he sought them out for lengthy conversations and turned on his best manners as a southern gentleman.
I could hardly believe my eyes and ears, though I determined to
make no subsequent comment but simply to accept his gracious
passing of the test as a matter of course. But my father could not
bear my silence and failure to commend him. Several days later
he called me aside and forced an assessment of his behavior as
he asked with a twinkle in his eye, "How do you think I did with
your black friends?" Obviously, he, too, was suffering from cultural ambivalence that was never resolved. In later years I would
overhear him say with some sadness to an acquaintance, "I lost
my son at Yale."

But my father would not have had it any other way. After my
graduation, he ceased exercising his man-of-the-house prerogative of offering the grace at mealtime whenever I was at home.
When I protested and argued that it was still proper for him to
say the blessing, he put me in my place as only he could do,
saying, "There's no point in having a dog and doing your own
barking!" From then on, I consented to pray whenever asked.

Between each year of seminary, I engaged in summer field
work that exposed me to two very different American communities and provided good comparative backdrops for what I would
face in the future in the South. I spent the first summer as a
"boy's worker" on the staff of a Methodist settlement house in
Ybor City, Florida, a part of greater Tampa. Ybor City was an
ethnic ghetto for cigar-making Cubans, many of whom did not
speak English and were having difficulty finding their way into
the mainstream of American life. I picked up a wonderful vocab-

ulary of Spanish curse words on the playground! Unlike Negroes, the physical appearance of Cubans did not make them conspicuous, and no segregation was imposed. They constituted the first trickle of the Spanish-speaking wave of immigration.

A second summer was spent in the West where I served as pastor of an isolated church in Bruneau, Idaho, once a cattle rustling hideout. The majority of the people there were Mormons, so I learned what it meant to be in a minority. I also had some contact with Indians; my first funeral was for an Indian woman who was more than one hundred years old. Like American blacks, Indians have also suffered deliberate barriers to prevent their entry into the mainstream of the nation, but, since Indians sometimes seek to protect their culture through isolation, comparisons are difficult to draw.

⊗

My education was to be extended. At the Yale graduation I was awarded a fellowship that made possible my planning a year abroad at the University of Edinburgh in Scotland. I coveted this opportunity as a legitimate excuse to live out of the country for a while, recognizing how valuable it would be to add a further distant perspective on my southern roots. Events moved quickly as I requested ordination and made plans for travel.

Because of my Yale divinity degree, my home church pastor had understandable anxiety about convening local Baptist clergy to constitute an ordination council. Predictably, social issues did not come up at all in the examination, for this was seldom seen as the business of the church. Also predictably, the one question that generated lively discussion had to do with my interpretation of the Bible as the authoritative Word of God.

Of the ordination service that followed, I draw a complete blank. I can account for this failure of memory as possibly reflecting a very dark cloud that descended on our family at about that time. We had learned that mother had a relapse of tuberculosis and would need to be sent to the state sanitarium in Columbia, some distance away, for perhaps a year. I left for Scotland and mother left for the hospital within days of each other, leaving Daddy in Greenwood with Rosa. I knew she would take care of him well.

Edinburgh is a beautiful old city, the Vatican City for Presbyterians. For some years a steady stream of students from the American South had gone there for graduate work in theology, for the word was out that Scotland produced superior preachers,

second only to whiskey as its number-one export. Just as Yale
had afforded an opportunity for me to understand myself as a
southerner, so being abroad enabled me to see more clearly what
it means to be an American. Here again, the prevailing image
was not too complimentary; many regarded "Yanks" as brash
and fun loving with very little depth. I learned quickly to say
thank you when people asked, "From what part of Canada do
you come?" for this meant that I had made a positive impression.

I found it difficult to settle down as a serious student. Even
so, I selected historical theology as my field of study and chose
a thesis topic that I wondered if I would ever complete. I was so
saturated with academics from six straight years in the classroom that I felt free now to devote more time to social life and
travel. Good theater and music were always available, and tickets were cheap, so I took advantage of the situation to broaden
my appreciation of the fine arts.

How vividly I recall attending a matinee performance of the
play *Anna Lucasta*, produced by an all-black American cast on
a Thursday in November. After the final curtain, the lead actress
stepped up to the footlights and said to the audience, "We are a
little homesick this afternoon, for today is an American holiday
when families get together for a thanksgiving feast." Then she
invited all compatriots in the theater to come backstage for a
party with the cast. Her sentiment and hospitality moved me
deeply. As I mingled socially with blacks on a stage set in Scotland, I knew that such an interracial Thanksgiving could never
have occurred in my South Carolina hometown. I too was homesick for Rosa's groaning table laden with turkey, sweet potato
casserole, and oyster pie.

The only other blacks I associated with in Edinburgh were
occasional African students who always had many questions
about the race problem in the United States. I found myself
surprisingly defensive and tempted to report conditions as being
better than they actually were. At that distance, segregation
seemed more contradictory to everything that Americans professed than ever before. I wanted to believe the truth of my claim
that the situation was gradually improving and that our caste
system would eventually end.

❦

The legacy of the war years was a recognition on the part of
many of my compatriots that the blatant hypocrisy of segregation had to be abolished. Martin Luther King, Jr., would later

hammer home the theme that the underlying philosophies of segregation are dramatically opposed to democracy and Christianity and that all the dialectics of all the logicians in the world cannot make them lie down together.

The evil of the system was surfacing for all to see. Southerners who for generations had prayed faithfully that Lord's Prayer petition "deliver us from evil" were about to see their prayers answered in unexpected ways.

Chapter 5

The New and Old South

"It's a good time to be a young preacher, lads; pulpit commit-tees are like that father in the parable of the prodigal son who said, 'Bring us a kid, and let us make merry with our friends,'" preaching professor Halford Luccock advised my departing sen-ior class at Yale.

Unfortunately, however, Southern Baptist graduates from Yale were not in such demand. Anyone schooled in a seminary outside the South became suspect as a liberal. A northern theo-logical education was tantamount to a betrayal of the southern church.

One of the few Baptist congregations in the Carolinas that transcended such provincialism was the Myers Park Baptist Church of Charlotte. Through a series of coincidental contacts, best accounted for as providential, I was invited to interview for a new position as assistant to the senior minister there in the fall of 1949.

Myers Park was a new congregation in the suburbs made up mainly of professionals and the nouveau riche who chafed under traditional Baptist puritanism. They were the country club set who no longer felt at home in a country-like congrega-tion. They yearned for something more sophisticated and intel-lectually stimulating. Under the creative leadership of George Heaton, Myers Park became widely known as an innovative, pace-setting church, especially for its unique family-centered emphasis on Christian education. Before eventually construct-

ing an authentic Colonial sanctuary, church functions were held
in Quonset huts on the church property and worship services in
the chapel of Queens College across the street. Myers Park
judged the success of its ministry by the biblical literacy of its
youth and its incredible record of holding families together—
boasting not a single divorce after eight years in a membership
of over one thousand! People called it "that liberal Baptist
Church," but as was usually the case in the late 1940s, the label
had little to do with matters related to race.

Dancing would be more controversial than the racial issue
in many Southern Baptist churches, but the members of Myers
Park quickly made it clear that their church was an exception.
The staff search committee asked, "Mr. Seymour, do you dance?"
My affirmative answer led to the logical follow-up question: "Can
you teach dancing?" to which I had to answer, "No." (In another
setting when someone asked, "Can Baptists dance?" I replied,
"Some can and some can't.") I got the job and spent a stimulating
year in what amounted to an internship under a mentor whose
style and administrative skills I subsequently emulated.

My primary debt to Myers Park was that it provided a point
of reentry for me into the South. I could go home again. Charlotte, although considered metropolitan by southern standards,
was not very large at the time despite continuing rapid growth.
The city liked to think of itself as a hub of the New South, but
racial patterns of the past remained intact with servants available for all affluent households. Sociologically, Charlotte was
unique, for instead of all blacks being confined to "the other side
of the tracks," some residential areas had rows of dwellings for
blacks sandwiched between the imposing mansions of upwardly
mobile whites, zoned for the convenience of having servants
nearby.

I do not recall race ever being a subject of controversy at
Myers Park or a concern of either pulpit or pew. (That would
change sharply in the next decade.) The controversy that did
emerge was not about blacks being admitted to the membership
but over the way non-Baptists could join the church. Ultimately,
though, the problem can be viewed as similar to racism because
it is rooted in people's hesitation to be inclusive of those who
differ from the norm.

At issue was the legalistic position of Southern Baptists that
required even professing Christians from other Protestant denominations to be put under the water (baptism by immersion)
before being welcomed into the membership. Heaton provoked

the conflict in a sermon by reporting a dream he had of David
Livingston walking down the aisle at Myers Park in response to
the hymn of invitation and the necessity of his saying, "I'm sorry,
Dr. Livingston, because you were baptized with only teaspoons-
ful of water and I with buckets full, you cannot belong to the
Myers Park Baptist Church." The spirited deacons' meeting that
followed extended until nearly midnight but failed to settle the
resulting division. Subsequently, Heaton avoided the unresolved
issue by welcoming scores of non-Baptists as candidates for baptism and simply delaying their immersion indefinitely.

Although relatively silent about racial problems, Myers Park
was the first Baptist congregation below the Mason-Dixon Line
to seek reconciliation with Northern Baptists by becoming dually aligned, thus bridging the split over the slavery issue that
occurred in 1845, more than a century earlier.

The congregation took pride in its splendid ministry to
youth. Newscaster Charles Kuralt was a product of that program. I recall a weekend retreat in the mountains when Kuralt
conducted the closing Communion service. Even then, the con-
versational poise for which he is famous today was evident. The
church also led the way among Charlotte congregations in spon-
soring and resettling Latvian refugees. I remember a conversation with one of them who was confused about the way we
related to blacks in this democratic country to which Latvians
had fled looking for freedom.

As for me, the people of Myers Park accelerated my matur-
ing in ministry as I flourished under their strong affirmation.
They enabled me to survive one of the most embarrassing incidents of my ministerial career. Flattered by the fact that the
senior minister assigned his pulpit responsibilities to me for the
entire month of August during his vacation absence, I assumed
that anything good enough for him was good enough for me.
Heaton always had an eye for comfort and had found a way to
get some relief from the oppressive summer heat while still
wearing his liturgical robe. He had installed a fan under the
pulpit and positioned it to blow cool air beneath the garment.
(Air conditioning had not yet come to the South. Without it, I am
confident there never would have been a New South. We southerners would still be rocking on the veranda with our mint juleps
in hand.) I presumed the same arrangement Heaton had without
realizing that our discrepancy in height would pose a problem
when I wore his robe. Instead of the fan working as anticipated,
it drew the hem of the robe back and forth toward the blades,

and in the middle of the sermon, the inevitable happened: My robe was sucked into the fan with a great commotion, threatening to chew me up before the congregation! Desperately, I yanked it out while trying to keep my mind on what I was saying. The choir, which had the best view of the mishap, was convulsed. The congregation, aware that something was happening, maintained typical southern politeness, sparing me total humiliation.

۞

After only a year in Charlotte, an opportunity came in 1950 to become pastor of a church of my own. It was a case of apostolic succession. The previous minister had been an upperclassman at Yale when I was there, and his recommendation opened the door for me. For three years following, I stepped out of the twentieth century to serve as the pastor of the Warrenton Baptist Church in a charming county-seat community of eastern North Carolina that had been bypassed by the modern world.

Founded in 1779, Warrenton is one of the older towns of the state. Graced by many beautiful antebellum homes, it still provides an easygoing lifestyle so typically southern. More than 60 percent of the people in the county are black, mainly farmers and descendants of the large plantation population. During the nineteenth century, Warrenton served as an educational center boasting several academies and female finishing schools, but its bright future was forfeited early in its history when the railway came South in the 1850s. Local citizens protested plans to route it through Warrenton lest it frighten the slaves!

The agrarian economy of the post-Civil War period forced the races to work together and to depend upon each other. When I arrived in Warrenton, racial relationships were generally cordial, but they were consistently confined to the separate-but-equal formula in regard to all public facilities. The emphasis, however, was always on the separation with a studied inability to admit any inequality.

During the fifties, Warrenton enjoyed a cocoon-like existence, convinced of its civility and not even remotely concerned about racial inequities or the possibility of trouble ahead. Like so many similar southern towns, whites prided themselves on their understanding of the Negroes and congratulated themselves on being so good to them. They honestly believed that everyone was completely comfortable with the situation just as it was and that blacks had no cause to complain.

The "good life" of this social climate was confirmed by a

feature article about Warrenton that appeared in *Life* magazine, "Life Goes to a Party," describing an annual social event hosted by local parents for the friends of their college-age young people. A clergy colleague who was the guest of the church for a week of preaching (no longer referred to as a revival), once observed, "The people here sin so graciously."

Initially, no one thought the new minister at the Baptist church would pose a threat to the domestic tranquility, but gradually people became aware of his unorthodox racial views and were quite defensive when anything was said from the pulpit or elsewhere to suggest that all was not well in Zion. I found one remarkable, sympathetic friend in the person of Bignall Jones, the editor of the *Warren Record*, the local weekly newspaper. He was a closet liberal, and I helped him come out. He relished the freedom of airing his progressive views with the new preacher in town, though his lonely voice did not threaten the citizenry who seldom took his views very seriously.

Another source of support surfaced among several men in the church who were veterans of the Second World War and had been abroad where servicemen of both races were billeted together. One of them, a deacon, confessed: "I never believed it could be so easy. I saluted Negro officers; I slept in the same barracks, ate at the same table, bathed in the same showers. What you've been saying is right. I am sure this is the way God intended it to be."

I learned quickly that the possibility of being an effective, forthright preacher was intimately related to also being an attentive, caring pastor. One cannot be a prophet in the pulpit if one fails to be a friend to people in their times of personal crisis. I learned that much also depends not only on what one says but in the way one says it. If a preacher mounts the pulpit like St. George getting ready to slay the dragon, he or she invites controversy. Whereas, if the tone comes across as protesting love and in the context of self-criticism, the minister is more likely to be granted a fair hearing.

I learned that people would respect one's integrity in espousing unpopular views even though they would have preferred the echoing of their own opinions. I felt good when, after a sermon on race, members would shake hands with me at the church door and say, "I didn't agree with what you said this morning, but you're my pastor, and it's your privilege to say it." Such response seeded hope.

Another valuable lesson learned in Warrenton is that, whenever possible, one should try to win the support of the power structure first before running the risk of stirring up the rank and file. I learned it while attending a statewide Baptist Student Convention in Charlotte. In order to have a pastoral visit with a number of our young people who were away from home on various college campuses, I invited them to meet me there and to be my guests at lunch. Several accepted, and one student arrived at the rendezvous place with a very dark friend, an American Indian from Pembroke. I quickly recognized a potential problem and concluded that the better part of wisdom was to take the group to a Chinese restaurant where we would likely be seated without the risk of a racial challenge. All went well until I returned to Warrenton where word had already spread that the pastor had "taken some of our young people out to eat with a nigger."

Very late on Sunday evening of that same weekend, there was a knock at the parsonage door. Three deacons had been dispatched to investigate the charge. I welcomed them and said I would also welcome an opportunity to have a called meeting of the entire board in order to clarify the matter and to share my full mind on the racial issue. I corrected the rumor that I had deliberately created the crisis by pointing out that the visitor in the group was an Indian, not a Negro as reported, but I made it clear that this would have made absolutely no difference in the nature of my response.

Two nights later the meeting took place at the church. I could feel the tension in the room as a dozen deacons waited for me to account for myself. I had decided that this was a choice time for me to speak my full mind and to "let it all hang out," irrespective of the consequences. For thirty minutes I stated as clearly and calmly as I could my judgment that segregation was an evil and untenable institution within the Christian community.

When I finished, there was a long silence. Finally, the first deacon to speak was Mr. A.S. Bugg, a millionaire farmer to whom many Warrentonians owed their livelihood. "Hrumpff," he began. "When I go out in the country to check on the niggers on my land, they sometimes ask me in to have a piece of pie with them, and I've done it. If I can have pie with my people, I don't see why my preacher can't go to lunch with one."

That ended the meeting! Mr. Bugg had spoken, and no one dared challenge his conclusion. I had been saved by an unexpected source of support from being rebuked or possibly fired, and the crisis had afforded a perfect opportunity to lay out precisely what I believed.

Another thing I learned in Warrenton about improving race relations is that one interracial meeting may be more effective in changing the attitudes of prejudiced people than countless sermons on the subject. As long as people are kept at a distance from one another, it is easy for them to believe the worst about one another. Also, when the primary contact whites had with blacks was with members of the servant class, it was hard for them to see beyond this relationship to acquire a more diverse and balanced impression. Many middle-class and professional whites seldom had opportunity to know their counterparts in the black community.

Actually, Warren County had a sizeable population of relatively well-off Negroes, many of whom owned their own farms. (Ironically, before the Civil War, there were also black freedmen in Warren County who were slave owners!) Sadly, the more privileged and professional blacks did not have the benefit of an educated black clergy and were thus, in effect, left unchurched. They did not feel at home in black congregations led by the unlettered and were not welcome to worship in white ones.

Interracial meetings helped bridge the separation of the races. The excuse for such gatherings was never to discuss racial issues per se but to solicit shared support for some worthy cause transcending both races. A nonthreatening purpose served as a catalyst for their coming together. Although mingling at a white church on a Sunday morning would have been unthinkable, no one objected to the church as a meeting place on a weekday for some broad-based community project.

One such cause was CROP (Christian Rural Overseas Program), an arm of the National Council of Churches designed to solicit the support of rural America in pledging a percentage of farm products for overseas postwar relief. This program generated considerable enthusiasm in Warren County, and for several years blacks and whites teamed up together to fill a railway car on behalf of their brothers and sisters abroad.

Rarely was a Negro invited to speak to an all-white organization. A report of what happened at one such meeting may have been apocryphal. I was told of a black gentleman being invited to a local women's club as a guest speaker, where, according to the account, there was a time for questions after he had completed his speech. One woman felt compelled to ask what she assumed was foremost on everybody's mind. Haltingly, she managed to inquire, "Would *you* like to marry a white woman?" Taken aback by the emotionally laden issue, the man simply smiled, bowed slightly, and said, "I thank you, my dear lady, but I am already married." There were no further questions.

A significant advantage of a clergyman in any community, and especially in the segregated South, is the freedom to move about at every level of its corporate life. The pastoral vocation is a passkey to places other people might never go. The role of the southern preacher has traditionally earned respect from everyone, and doors have stood open for the man of God to enter across racial lines. As the minister of the Warrenton Baptist Church, I felt free to call on the black school principal, to meet with black clergy, and even on occasion to enter a black home. I am certain now that such freedom of movement on my part raised suspicions among blacks about my motives, yet not surprisingly, whites seemed to regard such access as not only my privilege but as a communication link that could prove valuable to them. Thus, there was always an intrinsic danger of being used to advance the agenda of manipulative whites.

One place I was expected to go on a regular rotating basis with other local preachers was to the county unit of the state prison system. Just outside the Warrenton town limits was a facility for several hundred inmates, all black. They were housed there to maintain the area highways as forced laborers. Groups of prisoners could be seen all over North Carolina under the watchful eyes of rifle-carrying guards with an old school bus with barred windows parked nearby. Every third Sunday afternoon, I went to the camp to lead the worship service, a white parson with an all-black congregation.

My anxiety in meeting this responsibility became visible the first time I went there. I felt exceedingly awkward, if not presumptuous, to be in this position. Sensing what I was feeling, an old black man sidled up to me and whispered, "Preacher, don't be nervous. We'se people jist like everbody else, only we'se the ones that got caught." His remark set me at ease immediately, and I have never felt any intimidation in talking to prisoners since.

❧

The minister of a small church is expected to fill all the staff functions that would require multiple persons in a large congregation. In Warrenton, a primary claim on my time was a ministry to youth that I welcomed as an opportunity to influence their formative years. I succeeded in sending several of them to national Christian conferences where I knew they would associate with blacks as peers for the first time.

I also recognized the timidity of Sunday school literature for teens in discussing any controversial subject, so I sought more provocative resources to challenge their thinking. The denominational lessons addressed the pupils as if they were members of a white church only, never considering the existence of black Christians or the possibility that blacks and whites might be studying the material together. I tried to help our young people realize the impossibility of white and black persons growing up in a segregated society without acquiring strange feelings about one other. I tried to make them see that if we refuse to admit our own prejudices, we are likely to justify them by watching members of the other race suspiciously. I wanted these Christian youth to understand that here, as in other areas of life, reconciliation begins where there is a willingness to confess one's own sin.

One boy in the group had a father in the state legislature and a grandfather in the congressional House. Both men used their elected positions to perpetuate the mores of the Old South and simply assumed that their church had no quarrel with their efforts to uphold the southern oligarchy's agenda. This easy alliance of political and religious leadership was typical of the entire region.

In the face of criticism about my position on racial issues, I discovered the advantage of moving beyond my own personal opinions to quote from an authority accepted by the challenger. Obviously, the first line of defense was the Bible, and in particular, the New Testament. Blacks also soon learned that white opposition could be rendered speechless when they quoted Scripture, for no southerner was ready to quarrel with the Word of God. Quoting the Bible was to become one of the most potent weapons in the oncoming civil rights struggle.

What could be more pointed than verses like that one from First John? "If a man say, 'I love God,' and hateth his brother, he is a liar" (4:20). The most persuasive sermons on race were always documented with biblical references; no one wanted to be accused of not taking the sacred book seriously.

Next to Scripture were the official pronouncements and resolutions of the denomination. These, too, could be quoted effectively as a means of disarming the opposition. Surprisingly, as early as 1947, the Social Service Commission of Southern Baptists had managed to get the Convention to adopt a remarkably straightforward Statement of Principles at its regular session in St. Louis. The approval of this document probably proves that preachers are more willing to be liberal on controversial issues when they are far away from home. Even so, the landmark pronouncement provided a reference point for local clergy caught in conflict.

This Statement of Principles pledged "to conquer prejudice" and "to protest against injustices and indignities against Negroes." It even stated, "We shall be willing for the Negro to enjoy the rights granted to him under the Constitution of the United States, including the right to vote . . . " The statement added, "we shall pay him an adequate wage." The proclamation stopped short of saying anything about moving toward an inclusive church. Rather, it pledged to cooperate "in the building of *their* churches." This forward-looking statement provided an important point of reference for leaders in the local church. They could strengthen their position by reminding the congregation of their denomination's stand on the matter.

&

One of the pioneer groups in improving race relations in the South was the YWCA. In 1953 I accepted an invitation from the Charleston, South Carolina, "Y" to lead a Religious Emphasis Week. Arrangements had been made for me to address the student assemblies at several local white high schools where I spoke about American ideals and their incompatibility with accepted practices of segregation. A storm of reaction kept telephones ringing at the "Y," and it suffered a backlash of diminished support as both parents and school administrators protested my remarks. Thirty years later, a Presbyterian minister from Charleston, West Virginia, called to thank me for a pivotal experience in his life and in determining his vocational direction. He identified himself as one of those high school students who had heard me speak. This illustrates that seeds of change affecting racial attitudes may lie dormant for a long time before bearing fruit.

Experiences in several interracial conferences as the Warrenton pastor left a lasting impact on my perspective of what the South might become. One of these was in a most unlikely situation in a surprising place. The Reverend W.C. Laney, pastor of a white Baptist church in a textile village just outside Hickory, had succeeded in quietly integrating his congregation with a few Negroes, including a black choir director. Laney initiated what he called "Fellowship Meetings" and invited sympathetic clergy of both races to come as guests of his church where we shared meals and slept in the church building since there were no other facilities available to accommodate a racially mixed group. It seemed such a daring thing to do, yet no objection from outsiders interfered. These meetings continued year after year and served to expose participants to a level of interaction and candor rarely found anywhere else in the region.

Another similar one-time experience occurred under the sponsorship of the United Christian Youth Movement (UCYM), the national interdenominational organization for college students. A week's conference planned for Lincoln Academy, a struggling black school near Kings Mountain, attracted fewer than one hundred participants, many of whom were black. For the first time in my life, I found myself living in a fully desegregated setting designated for Negroes only. I felt as if I had entered a foreign country. The accommodations were austere, though the genuineness of the welcome and spirit of inclusiveness quickly dispelled the sense of being an outsider. A young black charismatic leader named Isaiah spoke about Christian love and justice without a trace of bitterness. He touched my life with the power of the prophet for whom he was named. We experienced some fear as we wondered whether local law enforcement officers were aware of our presence and how they might react to it. No crisis ensued, and the days together culminated in one of the most meaningful Communion services of my life. At dawn on the final Sunday morning of the conference, we literally kneeled on the lawn, facing the nearby mountain, and sang as we worshiped:

> Let us break bread together on our knees . . .
> When I fall on my knees with my face to the rising sun,
> Oh, Lord, have mercy on me.[1]

By the mid-fifties the first tremors of threatening racial change were beginning to be felt even in Warrenton. Word that the neighboring town of Henderson had employed a Negro policeman caused considerable consternation. The thought of giving to black citizens some sense of ownership of the law was an alien idea, and the possibility of a black man arresting a white man was still beyond contemplation. News about the integration efforts of the National Association for the Advancement of Colored People (NAACP) caused many to conclude summarily that this could only be a communist-front organization. By the spring of 1953, I began to sense that my honeymoon with Warrentonians was over and realized I had done well to survive so long. Also, in the back of my mind was the awareness of a Ph.D. thesis yet to be completed in Scotland. The thought of returning to an academic setting and going abroad again seemed more and more attractive.

I resigned from the church, and more than twenty years passed before I was asked back to Warrenton to speak. The occasion was a high school graduation. The person who introduced me apologized profusely for my unpopular ideas even then, saying, "We have not always agreed with our speaker tonight, but we love him."

I cherish the parting words in the editorial that appeared in the July 31, 1953, edition of the *Warren Record* when I left the community. I was able to feel that perhaps I had helped further understanding between races when Bignall, my editor friend, wrote: "Because of [Seymour's] sincerity . . . a liberality of views which at times has seemed shocking to some of his congregation . . . he has been tolerated by those to whom such views are anathema, and even, happily, some of these views have become accepted."

Chapter 6

Piety and Social Change

At first my pursuit of the Ph.D. at the University of Edinburgh was motivated solely to afford a legitimate excuse to spend time overseas. As I planned to return for a second year, I determined to become a recluse and complete the project. I knew it would be difficult, for I am a gregarious person by nature, and the lure of social life, plus the many cultural attractions of the old Scottish city, were ever present.

Generally the Ph.D. affords a passport to the teaching profession. I reasoned it would be to my advantage to have available this alternative career to a pastorate in case I found it impossible to survive in a local church. It never occurred to me then that this academic credential could also be a coveted asset for a pastor in a college or university town. In retrospect, I judge my graduate study to have been providential preparation for spending the remainder of my ministerial career in two churches, both intimately associated with institutions of higher learning. The doctor of philosophy degree enabled me to relate to professorial parishioners as an academic peer.

My thesis topic was in the area of historical theology. It focused on an eighteenth-century English Baptist preacher named John Gill. Gill was a rigid Calvinist whose well-known ministry coincided with that of John Wesley with whom he engaged in an ongoing public debate about evangelism and baptism. Gill wrote voluminously, and I chafed under the task of perusing his dry-as-dust material. My faculty advisor judged this to be a healthy response. Not only would I be forced to answer Gill's arguments, he said, but I would also benefit from the sharp contrast Gill provided to twentieth-century thought. Completing the dissertation was accomplished by painful, self-imposed discipline and a yearlong withdrawal from the world.

My ivory tower did not cut me off from news from home, however. Word from North Carolina was discouraging. Baptist chaplains at both Duke University and the University of North Carolina were being investigated for theological heresy, though it was the opinion of many people that the hidden agenda had more to do with race. The Baptist Student Union had become too liberal in its leadership, and it was easier to remove the chaplains on doctrinal grounds than to risk a controversy over integration.

Then, in May 1954, came the incredible good news. The Supreme Court had ruled in the case of *Brown* v. *School Board of Topeka* that having separate schools for blacks and whites was unconstitutional and decreed that the nation must move toward one integrated educational system "with all deliberate speed." Seldom have I been so proud to be an American. Here was concrete evidence, more compelling than anything I could have anticipated, to support my claim to British friends that the status of the Negro in the States was improving. Surely this landmark decision sounded the death knell for segregation! With one stroke of the pen, the Supreme Court had achieved what the churches had been powerless to accomplish for a hundred years.

Even as I rejoiced in the judgment, I could not imagine it being implemented in such places as Greenwood and Warrenton. What would it have been like to have gone to school with Rosa's sons, Frank and James L.? I found it difficult even to entertain seriously that possibility occurring in South Carolina and began to feel exceedingly anxious about the predictable recalcitrance that would follow. Now the fat was in the fire. The latent racism of respectable southerners would likely surface as never before. The public school system of the South, already the poorest in the nation, could worsen and might not survive. Even so, whatever the future held, I felt called to be a part of the process. I was eager to put the finishing touches on my thesis and head for home, though travel plans for the summer would delay my return until fall.

My mother (who now enjoyed good health again), an aunt, and a mutual friend arrived at Southampton to begin a grand tour of Europe. I met them in my English Ford Popular to fulfill my commitment as chauffeur, baggage boy, and tour guide for three whirlwind weeks. Then I drove back to Edinburgh one last time to learn that my thesis had been approved and my degree assured.

In midsummer I joined three seminary friends for the major travel adventure of my life: an attempt to follow the itineraries of the apostle Paul's missionary journeys, using the New Testament as our guide. We camped across the Middle East, consumed gallons of Kaopectate, and plotted our course over some of the world's worst roads. We pitched our tents amidst the ruins of Corinth, Philippi, and Ephesus, and then we drove across Turkey and entered Syria by way of the Cilician Gates. I never turn to the Letter to the Ephesians without remembering our dramatizing the protest of the Diana idol makers against Paul; we acted it out in the very same amphitheater in which it had occurred. At night, in the silence of the extensive excavated antiquity, we could still hear bull frogs chanting the ancient refrain: "Great is Diana of the Ephesians!"

Because of the Arab-Israeli conflict, it was almost impossible to travel into Israel from Jordan, but by a well-rehearsed procedure with official documents and the United Nations attendant, we succeeded in crossing the border for ten final days in the Holy Land before putting our car aboard ship to sail the Mediterranean back to Italy. Memories of that summer afforded a lifetime backdrop to biblical study.

Home at last. Every time I returned to Greenwood, Rosa would be standing in line to greet me. "Come, give me a hug," she would say, and then add, "You really is lookin' good, Mister Bo. I sho' is glad to see you."

Henceforth Greenwood would never seem the same. Emotionally I belonged there, but I was so out of step with the community in its racial views that I also suffered acute feelings of alienation. For several months I marked time with polite parlor talk and a minimum of conversation about the Supreme Court decision. I tried once to discuss the situation with Rosa, but it was very clear that she felt intimidated into silence. For her the repercussions of the ruling must have seemed incomprehensibly confusing. White people in South Carolina considered it rude to even bring up the subject; they acted as if it would go away if ignored. I had increasing doubt about my ability to adjust to another church in the South.

Then in 1955 an invitation came from a most unlikely place. The Mars Hill Baptist Church was a congregation adjacent to the campus of Mars Hill College, located in the heart of the North Carolina mountains near Asheville. More than 90 percent of the church's large membership came from the faculty and student body. At that time, Mars Hill was still a junior college with a thousand undergraduates and was one of seven educational institutions of higher learning supported by North Carolina Baptists. The church was without a pastor, and I was asked to preach there as a candidate for the vacancy. I had never been on the campus before and knew the school only by its conservative reputation.

With tongue in cheek, I agreed to supply the pulpit. Due to my preconceptions of the college, I was privately amused at even the prospect of being called to serve as pastor there. From a distance I had seen it as puritanical, straight-laced, and pietistic. I also knew that many of its students came from fundamentalist congregations. Surely a Yale seminarian at such a conservative school could lead only to trouble.

What I had not expected was the fierce independence of the pulpit committee. The Baptist State Convention had been concerned about the vacancy of the Mars Hill pulpit, and upon hearing of my visit as a candidate there, the state executive secretary warned the committee that it would be a serious mistake to consider me.

This served only to strengthen the committee's resolve to further explore my coming. I had made a good impression, and I had been graciously received. Sensing my reservations about the situation, a member of the committee, John McLeod, called me aside and whispered, "Brother Seymour, don't be afraid to come to Mars Hill. We have such a conservative reputation up here that you can do anything you want to do, and no one would ever suspect it."

It was true. In this remote mountain community, there was a core of committed people whose minds were open and who were willing to be led. Also, some of the traditional narrow-mindedness for which Mars Hill was known had caved in after World War II under the pressure of returning servicemen who refused to accept the parental-like authority that the college administration had habitually exerted over students. There had been a time when couples could not even hold hands on campus. Students alleged that if they were caught doing so, the dean of women would ask, "What are you saving for marriage?"

Although I received a unanimous call to the church, I accepted with some misgivings. I feared further interference from the denomination, for obviously the church would have to remain closely associated with the Baptist State Convention. On the other hand, where could one find another pulpit with such potential influence? Students flocked to the church. The balcony was the favorite place for courting because students knew that only the preacher could see what was going on there and that he wouldn't tell. This was before the days of student access to automobiles, so services were packed with young people twice on Sundays. On Wednesday evenings it was not uncommon for four hundred persons to show up for prayer meeting! I was hard pressed to prepare three major messages every week, but, by the grace of God, I not only managed to meet the multiple deadlines but felt exhilarated by the challenge.

Students did not know what to make of me. My own youthfulness and ability to talk their language gave me an edge, but my refusal to use the familiar phrases of fundamentalist theology left some puzzled and made others suspicious. Most of these young people had grown up in congregations where they were accustomed to a steady diet of evangelism and emotional exploitation. When I failed to measure up to their expectation of such pulpit fare, some students began to question the authenticity of my faith and put me on their prayer lists for special intercession. But a few quickly realized that I was appealing to their minds and eagerly gave their undivided attention, hungry for more.

Faculty and staff, including thirteen ordained clergymen in the congregation, offered enthusiastic support and seemed relieved to be spared nonstop revivalistic preaching. They understood the need of students to see the implications of the faith they had professed. For too long most of these young people had heard only the personal gospel and subscribed to a primary principle of pietism: that the eradication of any social evil begins and ends in evangelism. They assumed that problems like racial injustice would simply wither away if enough people were "won to Christ."

Professors also affirmed my insistence that personal consecration needed to be matched with intellectual competence. They were in agreement with my repeated contention that we are called to love God with our minds and that intelligent inquiry can lead only to God's truth.

From the outset, I let my racial views be known. A first sermon on the subject reflected upon the prejudicial implications of that question asked about Jesus: "Can anything good come out of Nazareth?" (John 1:46, RSV). I said that just as the people of Jesus' day had been ready to believe the worst about the Nazarenes, so were Americans ready to believe the worst about Negroes. I said further,

"Whether we like it or not, we are living in a new South, and a revolution is underway. . . . I know the subject is a sensitive one. . . . I know that prejudice is not only a sin that besets us; it is a sin we have felt forced to perpetuate in our southern surroundings. Yet I do not believe you would ever wish this pulpit to reflect the prejudices of our society. I believe you would always want your preacher . . . to speak the truth."

With the possible exception of Dr. Hoyt Blackwell, president of the college, who could see the handwriting on the wall about the eventual inevitable consideration of Negroes for admittance to the student body, the response was largely positive. He, too, agreed with me personally and acknowledged the validity of the ultimate goal, but he was caught in a Catch-22 situation. Like so many southern leaders, he was accountable to a constituency far from ready to welcome change, so he counseled patience and advised against pushing too fast.

Actually, the racial issue was not very threatening to Mars Hill, nor to many towns in the western mountain area, for few Negroes lived there. During the Civil War, pockets of the population had supported the Union cause. Probably no more than a dozen black families resided in Mars Hill, yet these were excluded from both the local white school and the white church. They worshiped in a place of their own and supported an itinerant preacher.

❦

You may have heard the story about the preacher who ran away with the church organist. That is precisely what I did. One of the first persons I met upon arrival at Mars Hill as a bachelor minister was a member of the music department faculty who also served on the church staff. Pearl Francis came from east Tennessee, that part of Appalachia that refused to secede from the Union during the Civil War. She had accepted a position at the college in order to be closer to home after having studied in Michigan and California.

We had a clandestine courtship. We saw each other primarily at staff meetings and all the regular services of the church. We

decided to make a public announcement of our marital inten-
tions on April Fool's Day in conjunction with an open house
already scheduled that Sunday afternoon at the new parsonage,
which many members of the congregation had not yet seen. My
mother and Rosa consented to come up from Greenwood as
caterers for the open-house reception, and they arrived laden
with silver trays, linens, cheese straws, and a choice assortment
of cookies. This was to be a first-class social event. They were
unaware of the impending news, and when we told them of our
engagement, I could not tell who was more pleased, my mother
or Rosa. Both felt they were gaining a daughter-in-law.

Pearl and I stood at the front door together where I introduced her as my fiancée to each of the guests upon arrival.
People could not believe we had pulled this off without local
gossips getting wise to it. A spontaneous celebration erupted as
all the guests graciously gave their enthusiastic approval and
congratulated their new pastor on his good fortune.

Pearl shared my racial views but not my politics. She came
from a strong Republican family. Since Mars Hill was now to be
her home, she decided to register to vote there. When she indicated her desire to register as a Republican, the registrar asked,
"Does your husband know about this?" (Madison County was
notorious in the North Carolina for its shady Democratic-con-
trolled party machine.) Then the registrar suggested she consider becoming an Independent.

Pearl and I married in June on the hottest day of the year
and sweltered in the LaFollette Baptist Church, which had no air
conditioning. My father was best man. I had neglected to tell him
that Pearl and I intended to recite our vows to each other without
being prompted by the minister. When I turned to her and began
to speak them, my father thought, "My God, he's forgotten he's
the groom and is taking the preacher's part!"

After our wedding, Pearl gave up her teaching in anticipation of a family. We were blessed with two children who arrived
close to one another: a son, Robert, and a daughter, Frances. We
were further blessed by being put in touch with a remarkable
Negro woman named Viola Barnett, whom we hired to help my
wife with our children. Her gentle, soft-spoken manner was
much like Rosa's and she cared for the children as if they were
her own. Viola exerted considerable influence among local
blacks as the matriarch of the Mount Olive Baptist Church. Sin-
gle-handedly, she had protested the injustice to Negro children
for whom there was no education available in the county beyond

their two-room grade school. She persuaded state officials to bus
them to Asheville, nineteen miles away. Black young people had
to travel that round trip daily to attend a segregated school because the law prohibited their enrollment at Mars Hill High.

After the Supreme Court decision mandating the shift to an
integrated school system, public education was put in limbo. "All
deliberate speed" was interpreted to mean at a snail's pace. Although the ruling was handed down in 1954, it was not until 1957
that any school system in the state began to comply. On July 24th
of that year, a full banner headline screamed across the front
page of the *Asheville Citizen*: "Three North Carolina Cities Take
Integration Step." The accompanying story reported that the
number of blacks admitted for all three districts in Charlotte,
Winston-Salem, and Greensboro added up to a grand total of
twelve!

Every effort was made to circumvent the ruling or to delay
implementation indefinitely. The prevailing climate of public
opinion throughout the South was "You shall not make us drink
of this cup." White citizens' councils and concerned citizens
groups mushroomed in nearly every community. Persons who
never would have considered identifying themselves with the
blatant racism of the KKK felt justified in joining these more
respectable versions of the same segregationist mentality.

Now the key phrase was "to preserve quality education." At
last whites were forced to acknowledge that the separate-but-
equal formula had been a fraud. They had to admit that many
Negro pupils would have difficulty competing with their white
peers at the same grade level for lack of comparable preparation.

Another rallying cry was "states' rights." People argued that
the federal government had overstepped its bounds and that
each state should be free to order its educational system in whatever way it chose.

A plan presented to the North Carolina legislature that attracted widespread endorsement (including that of the state
president of the Baptist Women's Missionary Union), was the
Pearsall Plan, bearing the name of its presenter. Under this proposal, parents dissatisfied with the mixing of the races in the
school their child normally attended could transfer the child to
a segregated one. If such action were not convenient, they could
then apply for a state tuition grant to attend a private, non-
sectarian school. Under the system proposed for allocating such

funds, the amount per pupil the first year would have amounted to only $135.

The sound of the church could scarcely be heard as citizens of North Carolina scrambled to frustrate the law of the land. The congregation at Mars Hill fully anticipated their pastor's judgment that "most of the people of North Carolina consider states' rights more important than human rights, regard law evasion as an acceptable course of action, and consider that which is easy and expedient preferable to that which is difficult but morally right."

The local Civitan Club asked me to discuss the Pearsall Plan at its next meeting. I pointed out that the plan was conceived and presented with only token consultation or consideration of Negro citizens. I warned that it provided a legal means for suspending the public schools, yet did so on the pretense of preserving them. The response of the club was unprecedented. Civitans unanimously voiced their disapproval of the plan in the following resolution which they released to the press: "In keeping with our creed as builders of citizenship, we, members of the Mars Hill Civitan Club, register our disapproval of the Pearsall Plan in that it threatens the imminent destruction of our public schools."

The statement received broad coverage in western Carolina and forced our state representative to make a public reply. He insisted, "The Pearsall Plan represents the total thinking of the best educational and legal minds in the state." Fortunately, the plan was declared unconstitutional and never put into effect.

My great hope was that Mars Hill College would be the first Baptist institution of higher learning in North Carolina to admit Negroes. It was ideally situated to lead the way. As has been said, compared to the situation elsewhere in the state, racial prejudice was not nearly so volatile in western Carolina where blacks accounted for such a small percentage of the population. I was convinced the community was ready and that both students and faculty would welcome the change. Not so with the trustees. It was clear that several members of the board would do anything within their power to block such a move. This left President Blackwell in a painful bind, for to offend trustees might mean losing essential financial support. So again he counseled patience—repeatedly.

Meanwhile, the Baptist State Convention had charged a Committee of 17 with making a careful study of ways by which the spiritual life of its seven colleges could be enhanced and deepened. In 1958 recommendations were brought back to the assembled body at its annual meeting.

Incredibly, the thirteen-page document did not make one single reference to the racial situation, nor did it even consider that the colleges had any obligation to North Carolina blacks. Instead, the report deplored evidence of drinking, gambling, and cheating on campus and urged more rigid regulations to prohibit undesirable conduct. (Apparently racial prejudice was not perceived as undesirable conduct.) The report also asked boards of trustees and administrators to study the basic principles of a Christian college. There was no indication that it had occurred to anyone who drafted the document that racial prejudice posed a problem for these institutions or that it was symptomatic of spiritual sickness.

Predictably, the report put strong emphasis on the usual expressions of pietism. The committee urged that there be morning watch, vesper services, religious focus weeks, and evangelistic crusades on every campus. It recommended that chapel attendance be required of every student.

In short, the report was tame and calculated. It dared not touch any controversial issue, for the bottom line intent was to motivate Baptists to gear up for a forthcoming financial campaign in support of higher education. Therefore, the promise of much-needed money could not be jeopardized.

The priority concerns of Baptists were further vividly revealed when the Convention voiced loud protest over the news that Wake Forest College had decided to permit social dancing on campus. The issue was hotly debated on the Convention floor. The trustee chairman explained that up until then dances had been scheduled off campus and were occurring, nonetheless, but without the benefit of any official sponsorship or supervision by the school administration. Then he made a fatal slip of the tongue. He said, "And that's where the rub comes in." The assembled Baptists broke out in extended raucous laughter. But the attention given the dancing issue while simultaneously neglecting the racial issue could not have been more revealing. Tacitly, North Carolina Baptists had made clear what the majority considered to be a more important matter of personal morality than racial prejudice.

☙

After it was clear that the administration of Mars Hill College was not ready to take the intiative to integrate, another strategy surfaced behind the scenes. An incident from the pre-Civil War history of the school suggested an alternate plan of action. It centered on the remembrance of a black slave who was affectionately referred to as simply "Old Joe." When the college was faced with a financial crisis occasioned by its inability to meet a mortgage payment due on its first building, a local farmer offered his slave as security for the debt. The offer was accepted. When the sheriff arrived, Old Joe was dragged off in chains to be held in the Asheville city jail where he remained for some days before finally being returned to his owner. Thus, the loss of the building was averted. This story had been told and retold by faculty members to every generation of students, and the most dramatic and tearful scene in the recurring historical pageant of Mars Hill's past romanticized the sacrifice of Old Joe for the school's survival.

The memory of this emotional episode sparked the new strategy. Suppose someone could find a qualified descendant of Old Joe who would apply for admission to Mars Hill College! How could even the most prejudiced trustee deny entry without an ugly reaction both on campus and in the press? A search proceeded quietly through the initiative of Bill Bagwell, a staff person from the American Friends Service Committee. Eventually, contact was made with Oralene Graves, who was a great-great-granddaughter of the slave Joe. She was a recent high school graduate with an ambition to further her education.

At a tense trustee meeting in Morganton in 1961, Oralene's application was formally presented. Every person present cast an affirmative vote. Thus, Mars Hill College repaid its long-standing debt of gratitude to its early benefactor and became the first private institution of higher learning in North Carolina to open its doors to blacks. On July 30, 1961, Oralene's picture appeared in the *New York Times* with an accompanying article headlined "Carolina College Admits First Negro." (By that time I was no longer the pastor of the Mars Hill Baptist Church, but I was present at this historic meeting as a newly elected trustee. I had the pleasure of witnessing this ironic twist to history become a reality.)

❧

By the end of the 1950s, nearly everyone in the southern church seemed to be running scared. As a college pastor, I was often invited to be a team member for religious emphasis weeks on other campuses. One such invitation took me to Louisiana

Tech at Rustin. When members of the Religious Focus Week team arrived to get instructions about scheduled events, the chancellor appeared to extend a welcome. His real purpose was to make sure no one said anything about the racial issue, for he bluntly decreed that the topic would be off-limits. Angrily, the entire team announced its refusal to participate in the planned activities and walked out. As we were packing our bags to return home, the administration relented and lifted its restriction. There were no further attempts to bridle the speakers.

Clergy all over the South were being drawn into the gathering storm. Many ministers faced the agonizing choice of speaking their minds fully and being fired or of being permitted to stay at the expense of their consciences. Some compromised their positions because of their families, while others forced martyrdom upon their loved ones. Occasionally, support groups surfaced to sustain pastors caught in the conflict. In North Carolina a small group of ministers organized under the innocuous title "The North Carolina Discussion Group." Announcements of these meetings could be made without giving anyone cause for alarm or arousing suspicion toward the preachers who participated.

The Home Mission Board of the Southern Baptist Convention, which later earned the reputation of being the most forward-looking agency of the denomination, also ran scared. Each year it published a mission study book to be read and discussed by the Women's Missionary Union all over the South. The 1958 title was *The Long Bridge*, an overview of the needs of Negroes in the South and the work in progress among them. As soon as the book appeared in Baptist bookstores, a thunderous opposition from churches prompted Courts Redford, the executive secretary, to a quick capitulation. He withdrew the book and authorized the destruction of several hundred thousand copies!

The women of the Mars Hill Baptist Church were indignant over this censorship. In their behalf, I wrote to Redford to express our dismay, saying, " . . . it would seem that the logical place to begin facing up to the acute problems of our society would be within the Church of Jesus Christ. . . . There is something badly wrong with our work when we can study the black man in Africa without a twinge of conscience and then three months later refuse to face up to our responsibility to the black man here at home."

My letter was answered by an editorial assistant in a telling, straightforward, sentence: "The fear of the administrators of the Home Mission Board and the Women's Missionary Union was that class discussions would lead to unpleasant debate and that what was said in debate would be charged to these agencies." A printed flyer, entitled "Withdrawal of the Book *The Long Bridge*," was included with a further explanation that was circulated convention-wide: When work on the book had begun, the subject matter had not been controversial, but recent developments had made the Mission Board unwilling to inject into the life of the churches a study that was so "fraught with the possibility of harmful debate and divisive discussion." According to the flyer, the book was being withdrawn because of the "unfavorable timing of the study."

❧

In North Carolina the State Convention created a new department called the Department of Interracial Cooperation. Many hailed this action as a positive step in the right direction. I made myself unpopular by expressing a minority opinion. I saw the agency as a way to take heat off the local church by suggesting that this new conduit was an appropriate way of keeping in touch with blacks, thus easing any need to make reconciling overtures to our brothers and sisters in our own backyards. When this new department promoted an annual observance of Brotherhood Sunday, I again raised a critical voice. Is once a year enough? Surely every Sunday should be Brotherhood Sunday! Brotherhood was not something you could put on a church calendar for a single day's emphasis—like the annual stewardship sermon—and then be done with it.

Despite my reservations about this new agency of the Convention, I must acknowledge that it was a source of much good and generated increasing trust among black and white Baptists in North Carolina. The first executive of the department was Dr. W.R. Grigg. He was a genial, rotund man whose premature graying gave him the appearance of Kentucky's Colonel Sanders. W.R. loved to tell the story of being introduced by a black pastor who concluded his remarks by saying, "and his heart is as black as ours."

It was Grigg who introduced me to some leaders of the General Baptist Convention, which is the separate black counterpart to the State Baptist Convention. I was invited to preach at their annual meeting and chose the topic "When Segregation Seemed Sacred," based on that passage in Acts in which God revealed to Peter that his refusal to associate with Gentiles was wrong. I drew a parallel between Peter's subsequent vision and

the vision of many that the "unnatural barriers we have built up
between us must be removed."

I continued,

> The vision may come in any number of ways. For some it has
> come as they have contemplated the inconsistencies of segrega-
> tion practices and the democratic principles upon which our
> country is built. Others have recognized the irrationality of our
> prejudices—the way whites cut themselves off from Negroes as if
> they were unclean and then employ them to prepare their food
> and care for their children; the way we refuse to sit next to them
> on a bus but don't seem to be bothered by standing next to them
> in an elevator. It doesn't add up.... Clearly Jesus considered every
> human being to be a child of God and mingled freely among them
> all.... Surely there can be no genuine brotherhood where people
> are legally required to live apart from one another.

The sermon elicited an ovation, but then an angry voice
from the audience demanded the attention of the chair. "I want
to know whether this white preacher would say to his own people what he has said to us today." How relieved I was to be able
to reply that I had preached the very same sermon, word for
word, at the Mars Hill Baptist Church a few weeks previously.

On a summer Sunday in 1958, four strangers appeared in the
congregation, three men and one woman. They were a pulpit
committee and founding members of a Baptist church being
organized in Chapel Hill where the main campus of the University of North Carolina is located. The foursome had come to
invite me to consider becoming their first pastor. They had been
easily recognized as a pulpit committee by a member who observed later that day, "In Mars Hill a woman doesn't come to
church with three men."

This was an agonizing decision. I had found unexpected
freedom in Mars Hill and had been exceedingly happy in my
ministry. I had also found my wife there and welcomed two
wonderful children into the world, yet the opportunity to be on
the ground floor of a new and innovative church in a university
setting was compelling.

Pearl and I decided this could be our primary life work. We
accepted the call and left the large, multistaffed Mars Hill congregation to go to a fledgling fellowship of just over forty persons

who had pooled their limited resources to purchase a parsonage and a piano.

The move coincided with the commencing of the turbulent sixties. For the next thirty years I would be the first and only pastor of a remarkable congregation, the Olin T. Binkley Memorial Baptist Church, in one of the South's leading liberal communities, Chapel Hill.

Chapter 7

The Church Challenges Culture

Viola Barnett agreed to make the trip to Chapel Hill with us and to stay until we were settled. We anticipated no problem in having a Negro woman live with us as long as the neighbors understood she was a paid servant. However, we did anticipate the problem of finding lodging for her when we stopped en route overnight.

I had written a clergy friend in Greensboro to ask if he knew a motel manager who would be sympathetic to our need and who would permit Viola's sharing a room with my wife and infant daughter. His answer assured us that he had arranged an accommodation at a reputable place in the center of town. We arrived late in the day and were exhausted from long hours of packing and traveling with fretting children and a restless collie dog. The journey had seemed interminable; it was before Interstate 40 bypassed all the towns. When I entered the motel office, the man behind the counter was all smiles in anticipation of our arrival. He seemed pleased with himself for being so considerate. Then he explained, "I have put an army cot in the furnace room for the Negro woman." I was dumbfounded. How could he have so completely misunderstood?

I replied sternly that this would not do. "If anyone sleeps in the furnace room, it will be me," I said. Shaken by my ingratitude, he protested at first, but then he reasoned that, if my wife really needed Viola, perhaps it would be all right for them to share a room after all.

This was an ominous beginning to negotiating the racial complexities of the decade ahead.

ॐ

The hill to which we had come in 1959 was very different from the hill we had left behind. At Mars Hill the Baptist church was at the center of community life; in Chapel Hill, it was only peripheral. At Mars Hill I had to hold reins on religious fervor; here I had to be assertive. Mars Hill College expected the preacher to pray with the team before athletic events; here games were won without benefit of clergy.

By Mars Hill standards, Chapel Hill seemed large, but people called it a village. Less than seven thousand students were enrolled in the university at the time; the number would increase to over three times that in the years ahead. The community was hard-pressed to provide services for such rapid growth. Electric, water, and telephone utilities that were originally built, owned, and operated by the university for the entire community were eventually sold to the private sector.

Chapel Hill has managed to keep its Camelot-like charm. It is the oldest state-owned university in the nation, with eighteenth-century buildings lovingly preserved. Streets meander off in all directions into heavily wooded neighborhoods where azaleas and dogwoods stage a spectacular show every spring. The campus is blessed by the shade of large oak trees that make it an inviting place even on hot summer days. The centerpiece and symbol of the university is an old well.

The University of North Carolina pioneered in making definitive studies of the southern region. The work of sociologist Howard Odum drew attention to the school as a pace-setting institution. Academic achievements and rankings with other comparable places of higher learning have always been impressive, but its liberal reputation in terms of racial issues at the beginning of the 1960s was more fiction than fact. Former university president Frank Graham, who also served North Carolina as a United States senator, is credited with comparing Chapel Hill to a lighthouse. A lighthouse sends its strong beam into the far distance, but it can be very dark at the lighthouse base.

Culturally, the town was very southern. The university community accepted segregation in stride and without challenge until change was forced upon it by the federal government. Negroes lived in one section of Chapel Hill and served the cam-

pus as cooks and janitors with low wages. Restaurants were open
to whites only. The local movie theater did not even provide a
balcony for blacks. Negroes and whites were worlds apart here,
just like everywhere else in Dixie.

Surprisingly, the First Baptist Church was the black congregation. New arrivals in town sometimes went there by mistake,
assuming it was the church that whites attended. The white congregation attended the Baptist Church at Chapel Hill, a large
building at the very center of town with huge columns out front,
like a classic Greek temple. When it became known that a new
Baptist congregation was about to be organized in 1958, the
established church changed its name to the University Baptist
Church, fearing the new congregation might preempt the name.

Local black public schools were so inadequate that graduates legitimately could be denied admittance to the university
because they were simply unqualified. Prejudice dictated community mores as if they were climatically controlled. This was
the South, the Old South, and this was the way southerners lived.

The founding of the Olin T. Binkley Memorial Baptist
Church occurred for several reasons. Primarily, the founders
realized that Chapel Hill was about to experience a steady period
of growth, and they were motivated to organize the congregation
to make room for the new people. Furthermore, charter members had become restless in the existing Baptist establishment,
especially in its reticence to offer leadership in the area of race
relations.

The captivity of the Baptist Church at Chapel Hill to traditional racial practices could not have been more vividly revealed
than in its response to the unexpected appearance of Negroes on
a Sunday morning in the mid-fifties. A Conference on Religion
in Life (CRIL) was occurring on campus, including students
from both races. Everone attending was invited to worship with
nearby congregations.

A mixed group of black and white students, including the
daughter of the executive secretary of North Carolina Baptists,
appeared at the Baptist Church. The chairman of the deacons
met them at the door and asked angrily, "What are you coming
here for?"

Undeterred by this hostile reception, the students entered
the sanctuary and were seated. Then the deacon chairman came
down front and called an immediate meeting of his board to

consider how to handle the situation while the congregation waited and the service was delayed. Nearly fifteen minutes passed before the singing of the first hymn. Then the chairman returned from the meeting, summoned his family, and left the service. He had been overruled by other deacons who concluded they could not ask anyone, not even Negroes, to leave God's house.

Later a compromise was reached. In the future the Baptist Student Union would be free to invite Negroes to functions in the basement fellowship hall, but since the church as a whole was not yet ready to formulate a position on race, Negroes would not be welcomed upstairs in the sanctuary. This decision was made in response to a recommendation from the church's Committee on Interracial Relations in which ecclesiology won out over theology, as indicated by the following excerpt:

> Two questions seem at issue. The first is the interpretation of the Christian ethic and its application to the race problem. The second is the question of church democracy which has from the beginning been a distinguishing characteristic of Baptist polity. If the Christian ethic is interpreted and applied as some think it should be, such an action will run counter to the democratic principle if it is honestly opposed by a majority. If it is opposed by a sizable minority, it may be the cause of a schism in the church. . . . [Therefore], this committee does not recommend that our regular services assume an interracial character.

Thus, a further reason for organizing the Binkley congregation was to make it unmistakably clear that the Christian fellowship is meant to be open to everyone. This understanding was foremost in the minds of the charter members from the outset. Yet, surprisingly, the founding documents are not as precise in addressing the racial issue as might have been expected.

The affirmation of faith declared: "We believe that God created man in his own image and made of one blood all nations of men to dwell on the face of the whole earth." And the church covenant added: "We agree to recognize the dignity and sanctity of every person, regardless of position or prestige, reflecting thereby our belief in the brotherhood of man; and to try to apply the teachings of Jesus in our ethical relationships in all walks of life."

Well and good, but such phrases were hardly earthshaking. The word "race" does not even appear here, much less any specific reference to Negroes. Southerners who were accustomed to such broad, general statements had the uncanny ability to process them mentally without any awareness of their relevance to local situations. In fact, several families later joined the new congregation in the mistaken assumption that this group was moving to the suburbs to escape the racial issue!

I had no doubt about the solid commitment of the founders to the principle of the inclusive church. When I met with them prior to accepting their call, we faced the race issue head-on. No one thought the matter could ever be a source of controversy in the emerging fellowship.

Furthermore, the church had chosen a name intended to convey its liberal position on the matter. Dr. Olin T. Binkley was then the dean of nearby Southeastern Seminary (where he would soon be named president) and a former professor of Christian ethics at Southern Seminary. He was held in high esteem by Southern Baptists and was well known for his open and progressive spirit. As a young man he had been pastor of the Chapel Hill Baptist Church, and he had also taught at the university. Local families remembered him as a forward-looking leader.

❧

In January of 1959, just before my arrival on the scene and only three months after its organizational service, Binkley Church welcomed its first Negro member. It happened quietly and without fanfare. George Grigsby was a freshman at the university from a small town, Holly Springs, just south of Raleigh. He was a pleasant, soft-spoken lad, who seemed very comfortable in a predominantly white group. By this time, several dozen Negroes had been admitted to the university student body in response to a court order. The first few undergraduate blacks had arrived in 1955.

The university granted permission to Binkley Church to hold its worship services in Gerrard Hall, an old building at the center of the campus. The chancellor, William B. Aycock, made this facility available to a series of new congregations, for he recognized a need for new churches to accommodate the expanding student body. Gerrard Hall had the appearance of a New England meeting house. It was constructed originally to serve as a chapel for university students at a time when even students on a state campus were expected to attend regular worship events. An inscription over the doors asks this biblical question of all who enter: "What doth the Lord require of thee, but to do justly, and to love mercy, and to walk humbly with thy God?" (Micah 6:8).

This campus location was uniquely situated for attracting black students to Binkley's faith family. Because the religious persuasion in the South is so homogeneous, we jokingly said, "Negroes from North Carolina have to be either Baptists or Methodists or somebody's been tampering with their religion." We intentionally reached out to them with a cordial welcome. Many came, and with them a contingent of sympathetic white students who were pleased by the novel experience of worshiping in an integrated congregation.

Five months after George Grigsby became a member, a news story appeared on the front page of the May 8, 1959, edition of the *Durham Morning Herald*, headlined: "Negro Joins White Church." I telephoned the editor and asked if he usually gave dated news such prominent exposure.

Now that the word was out, predictable repercussions followed. Hate mail outnumbered supportive correspondence two to one. One letter read: "I was shocked and grieved when I saw that one who professed to be a Christian . . . had committed such a sinful thing as to take a Negro in your church. I'm a Baptist and believe the teachings of God, and He taught segregation from cover to cover." Another, with an altogether different tone, came from as far away as Winston-Salem. The writer congratulated us for accepting a Negro into the church, saying, "I think it is a demonstration of genuine Christianity."

Sit-ins at lunch counters began in Greensboro in 1960 and spread throughout the South. These soon led to kneel-ins at churches. In some places, including such prominent congregations as the First Baptist Church of Atlanta, blacks were carried out bodily and were threatened against returning. Many white worshipers felt a sense of urgency to formulate membership policy before blacks put them to the test. They activated dormant membership committees, and instead of voting immediately on those who came forward to join (as was the custom), some churches now required every prospective member to meet with the deacons first to ascertain whether their motives for affiliating were pure. By such procedures, blacks could be challenged in a way whites had never been screened previously. When Negroes arrived for worship at one church, a greeter accused, "If you were Christians, you wouldn't be here!"

In addition to the use of Gerrard Hall for worship, the Binkley congregation rented an old house nearby to provide a place for the nursery, the church office, and various congregational activities. Several students lived in the house and assisted with janitorial chores in lieu of rent. George Grigsby requested permission to do this, and it was granted. Recurring rumors reported the unhappiness of nearby neighbors upon hearing that a Negro resided there.

Meanwhile, the magazine section of the March 24, 1963, edition of the *London Times* featured a photograph of our congregation at worship with blacks and whites sitting together. The accompanying article reported what was happening in Chapel Hill as evidence of a new America in the making.

❧

An advantage of participating in the organization of a new congregation is the ability to start out with clearly stated theological and ethical positions that tend to make the members more compatible. Only people who are sympathetic to the church's posture are likely to be attracted to it. The heavy weight of tradition does not stand in the way of moving out in new directions.

One of the first decisions made by the Binkley founders was that the congregation should be a part of the ecumenical movement, not just spiritually, but structurally. To do so meant going against the mainstream of Southern Baptist life. It was exceptional for any Baptist church to be affiliated with a council of churches, whether at the local, state, or national level. The new congregation unanimously requested admittance as a participating constituent of the North Carolina Council of Churches. Out of more than three thousand Baptist congregations in the state, fewer than a dozen such requests had been received! The Council, which normally grants membership to denominational bodies only, graciously established a special category of membership to include these atypical local Baptist congregations.

The affiliation led to an unexpected controversy. Earlier, the Binkley constitution had established two kinds of membership: full members, who had been baptized by immersion; and associate members, who had been baptized in other ways. Acceptance of the Binkley Church into the North Carolina Council of Churches posed a glaring inconsistency. How could we be "equally yoked in Christ" within the larger fellowship of the church while refusing full membership at the congregational level to those who joined from denominations with a different mode of baptism? Here was a replay of the Myers Park in Charlotte dispute with strong feelings expressed that at times seemed irrational in their intensity.

Unfortunately, most Baptists, as well as non-Baptists, see baptism by immersion as the primary distinction of the Baptist faith. In fact, the original issue had nothing to do with the method of baptism but was a question of who should be baptized—infants or believing adults. The principal concern was the assurance that every person admitted to the church had made his or her own personal profession of faith. Obviously, this concern is addressed in those communions that baptize infants by the follow-up rite of confirmation, but many Baptists have a hard time conceding this. For them, immersion has become an idol, a sacred ritual without which one cannot be considered fully approved by God.

I was dismayed by the explosive divisiveness of this issue. At a time when Binkley members should have directed their energy to more relevant matters, church conference after conference failed to resolve the conflict to everyone's satisfaction. Finally, a vote was taken, and the church, in effect, became an open membership Baptist church—but it did so at the cost of several unhappy families withdrawing their affiliation.

Relieved to have this crisis behind us, and feeling the issue finally had been resolved, we were then faced with the very same controversy all over! This time it was from another source. Although Baptist ecclesiology respects the autonomy of the local congregation, each church relates to other Baptist ones in a given geographic area through associations. Binkley was supposed to belong to the Yates Baptist Association with headquarters in nearby Durham. This was the association that had purchased the property in Chapel Hill where our church would eventually be located. Everyone assumed our admission would be automatic.

It was not to be. When leaders learned of the open membership policy, they voted to delay Binkley's application for a full year in order to study the implications. No one ever publicly mentioned the fact that Binkley now had a Negro member, but it was clear even at the time that this carried more weight in the controversy than anyone was willing to admit. In effect, to receive our church would have meant integrating the association. Again the *Durham Morning Herald* (October 27, 1960) gave the incident a full headline across the top of the second section: "Binkley Memorial Rejected by Yates." The final paragraph of the news story was telling: "Shortly after the church was organized here, it became the first church in the Yates Association to admit a Negro to membership."

Rejection did not disturb the congregation. If anything, it served to strengthen its commitment both to the ecumenical movement and to racial inclusiveness. Binkley Church has not been admitted to the association to this day, and so, as its pastor, I could stay away from innumerable associational meetings with a clear conscience.

❧

After the success of the Montgomery, Alabama, bus boycott, everyone in America knew the name of Martin Luther King, Jr. In the South many saw him as just another troublemaker. Soon he was to be labeled the pawn of Robert Kennedy whom many southerners would accuse of arrogantly forcing integration on the South. Southerners, especially Baptists, were also slow to warm up to presidential candidate John F. Kennedy. From the beginning of his campaign, we were warned about a Roman Catholic conspiracy to take control of the government.

In September 1960, Martin Luther King, Jr., came to Chapel Hill. The ministerial association sponsored a luncheon in a member clergyman's home to provide for us a private visit with him. That day stands out vividly in my memory. I had expected to meet an angry crusader, but instead, I found myself in the presence of a soft-spoken, gentle man to whom I readily surrendered my total admiration. King spoke with a consuming sense of destiny as he assured us of the ultimate triumph of his cause.

That evening King was scheduled to address students on campus. Hill Hall was packed with standing room only. The assembled group was loud and boisterous, clearly indicating that many had come only to jeer. When King appeared, the applause and hooting were intermingled, but he did not seem at all rattled by the obvious hostility of many in the audience. Amazingly, before the evening was over, he had everyone listening intently and succeeded in disarming even the most belligerent questioners. I was proud of the fact that Martin Luther King, Jr., was a Baptist preacher.

King spoke again the following night at the Baptist Student Union, which scheduled its regular meetings at the University Baptist Church. There he had a more sympathetic hearing, but in keeping with the new church policy about Negroes on the premises, he spoke in the fellowship hall, downstairs.

❧

A black friend from the Cameroons wanted to visit us in Chapel Hill. He and I had become acquainted in Europe, and now he was touring the United States. Of course I encouraged him to come, but his presence made me all the more sensitive to the restrictions imposed by our segregated town.

After several days of having all our meals at home, we decided to risk dining out at the only restaurant in Chapel Hill reported to be open to everyone. The Ranch House was a fine place to eat, established by a refugee family from Vienna. It was a popular place both for local people and for out-of-town visitors. The hostess welcomed us and we were seated promptly without any apparent awkwardness. Once seated, however, we felt stares directed towards us from all sides that were discomforting in their penetration. We placed our order and then waited for a full hour before any food was forthcoming. I became increasingly nervous as we sat there. I am confident the management was not responsible, but evidently our waiter was not sympathetic to the restaurant's "serve everyone" policy. My friend's visit made me realize the near impossibility of persons of color finding their way around in the South.

Both Rosa and Viola visited us in Chapel Hill on a number of occasions; they would arrive via Greyhound Bus. They always looked forward to coming, especially to see our growing children. Although we welcomed them as house guests and tried to relate to them as such, it was clear that they were not quite certain what their role was meant to be. Inevitably, they gravitated to the kitchen, and, in effect, became live-in servants, eager to assist Pearl in all the domestic chores. They were obviously pleased to observe other black persons in the congregation when they accompanied us to worship, and members of the church consistently welcomed them warmly. It was always a little disconcerting to me, however, to see Rosa before me from the pulpit, for invariably, she would be wearing one of my mother's hand-me-down hats. Mother loved hats, especially those made with large floral designs, and these hats became conversation pieces for both women.

❧

Racial incidents multiplied on every front.

Chapel Hill's Carolina Theater was open to whites only. When it advertised the coming of a film version of *Porgy and*

Bess, blacks asked for permission to see it, but the manager denied their request. Then teachers from the Negro school appealed for a special showing for their pupils on a Saturday morning. Once more, the answer was a flat no. When the community was informed of this indignity and the management's refusal to arrange a viewing even for blacks only, protests from whites were also raised. Binkley Church diaconate minutes note: "Some discussion of the role our church should play in the current efforts to desegregate the movies resulted in no concrete plan of action at the moment except to boycott the movies."

Chapel Hill Negroes often drove ten miles to Durham to see a film. Theaters there offered the traditional seating arrangement with whites downstairs and a separate entrance for blacks to reach the balcony. Some whites shuddered at the very thought of sitting next to a Negro in the dark. Managers justified the separation by explaining that blacks were often dirty and that their white patrons needed to be protected from those who practiced poor hygiene. No one ever heeded the suggestion that if this were really the case, it would make much more sense to simply check all customers for cleanliness. A representative of the health department could be stationed at the door to decide where patrons should be seated, irrespective of race, depending upon their state of personal acceptability according to the screening standard.

❧

Diaconate minutes noted a deacon's insistence that Binkley find ways to do more toward improving the Negroes' community status. One concrete proposal put forward was that everyone present covenant to pay adequate wages to their domestic help.

Another sign of the times was a hubbub over a Negro child who had signed up to play on a Little League softball team. Several white parents demanded his removal, but the boy's parents were adamant in their refusal to withdraw their son from the program. Sadly, the matter was resolved by simply cancelling the entire summer activity. Angered over this injustice, a member of Binkley Church organized a new league that was supported in part by the ministerial association, and 20 percent of those who played were black.

Despite reservations about setting aside only one day as Brotherhood Sunday, Binkley Church chose to observe it by sending designated members of the congregation to visit local Negro churches. Also, we negotiated an invitation for our choir

to sing at the St. Joseph's African Methodist Episcopal Church in
Durham. In the Old South, whites often listened to black choirs,
but white choirs never sang in black churches.

New line items began to show up in the annual church budget. One such item was "The General Baptist Convention," the
state-wide black Baptist body. Another item was "Burned
Churches in the South." Some rural church buildings in the deep
South had been torched, and, in most cases, there had been no
insurance to cover the loss. These budgeted items were more
significant for what they symbolized than in the actual amount
of money involved.

ॐ

Chapel Hill had an active group of United Church Women.
As has been the case often, church women were generally ahead
of the men in their social service involvements. As an organizational auxiliary to the North Carolina Council of Churches, the
United Church Women's primary continuing project was to improve the status of migrant workers who came through the state
every harvest season. The majority of these laborers were black,
traveling north from Florida. A photograph of a local Negro
child and our daughter, Frances, seated amidst a huge collection
of stuffed animal toys, appeared in the *Chapel Hill Weekly* to
solicit further gifts and funding for migrant families.

Pearl and I were pleased by the prospect of rearing our
children in Chapel Hill. We thought they would have a better
chance of growing up with less prejudice. Furthermore, there
were many opportunities for them, such as access to swimming
lessons at the university pool and a school system superior to
most in the state, although just as segregated as anywhere else.
Moreover, we enjoyed a greater sense of freedom as a family.
Our life in the parsonage at Mars Hill was like living in a fish
bowl, whereas in Chapel Hill people expected little more of the
minister's family than anyone else. Folk were more likely to
keep an eye on the children of the many resident psychiatrists
than those of the preachers to see how they turned out.

ॐ

Two months after Martin Luther King's visit, I attended the
annual convention of North Carolina Baptists in Asheville.
King's hope for the future was contagious, and I still felt awed
by his courage. I contemplated what actions Baptists might take

to push further toward integration. Asheville would be a preferred place to take a bold step forward since so few Negroes lived in the surrounding area.

Aware of what was concurrently happening behind the scenes to open the doors of Mars Hill College to Negroes, I decided this would be a good time to challenge the state convention to move with all deliberate speed in removing the color barrier from all seven of its academic institutions. Earlier, a Committee of 21 had requested that trustees of these colleges study the matter, but years had passed with no action forthcoming. Additional leverage now lay in the fact that every Southern Baptist seminary had disavowed segregation and several Negroes were already enrolled.

When the messengers (delegates) approved a proposal for a major long-range effort to raise $45 million for Baptist colleges and to expand facilities to handle 50 percent more students, it seemed unconscionable to proceed without facing the moral ramifications of segregated Christian education. I therefore presented a resolution calling for a request that the trustees of the Convention's seven Baptist colleges implement integration with all deliberate speed. The resolution hit the convention like a bombshell. Some complained that the timing could not have been worse due to the prior action on the fund drive. The resolution made headlines in every major newspaper in the state. Convention procedure required that resolutions be referred to a committee for consideration before being brought back for action on the convention floor. As anticipated, it was not returned. No action was taken.

A satirical editorial in the December 5, 1960, edition of Wake Forest's student newspaper, *Old Gold and Black*, advised: "Before we can go back to pretending there is no race problem to be dealt with, perhaps we should shush Dr. Robert Seymour, who'll probably attempt to continue his provocative insistence that we open our doors to Negroes . . . Perhaps the best recourse is just to ignore Seymour as the convention tried to do."

Nonetheless, each of the institutions subsequently lowered the racial barrier in the next few years. Ironically, Chowan College, the eastern North Carolina school that was initially the most resistant to the change and had voted to exclude Negroes, today has a 30 percent enrollment of blacks, the highest percentage of minority participation at any traditionally white institution of higher learning in North Carolina!

ᘔ

Meanwhile, back in Chapel Hill, pressure was mounting to desegregate the public schools. As in most communities in the state, the school board had expended considerable energy to delay implementing the Supreme Court mandate. In fact, tax dollars were being spent in a local court case to keep a black teenager out of the white junior high school. His parents had sued for his right to attend the school closest to their home. It would have brought a black pupil into an all-white classroom for the first time, but the action failed. School authorities insisted they needed more time to come up with a comprehensive, long-range plan.

Mixing the races in the public schools was a potentially divisive issue for every congregation in town, yet there was a broad base of support within the Christian community as a whole for immediate integration. In order to circumvent controversy in any particular church by pushing congregants to take a stand on the matter, a way was provided for them to work together on an ecumenical basis. Thus, those who were ready to welcome the change could push for it while others more reluctant need not.

A task force convened as the Fellowship for School Integration. It was a single-issue organization with participants from nearly every church in town. The Fellowship drafted a number of proposals for the school board to consider and exerted unrelenting political pressure upon each elected member. There was concern that any transition to an integrated system be orderly and peaceful and that the procedural details be spelled out clearly, well in advance. Any plan that placed the burden for requesting admission to an integrated school on the student or parents, rather than on the school board, would be seen as grossly unfair.

The clergy found a way to remove the edge of fear from young children for whom racial mixing might seem strange and unsettling: an interracial Vacation Bible School. All elementary school age children were invited, but no one was pressured to take part. Nearly two hundred children showed up, one third of them black. It was a huge success.

The only awkward moment occurred when a leader suggested to a group of five-year-olds that they dramatize their favorite stories. "Which story would you like to act out?" she asked. "Little Black Sambo," a child answered. Flustered for a moment, the teacher felt greatly relieved when a white child begged to play the part of Sambo!

My own children, Robert and Frances, were approaching school age and would be assigned to nearby Glenwood School. I was caught off guard when a neighbor came to our door with a petition to block integration there because of what it would allegedly do to property values in the area. He went away obviously miffed by my refusal to sign.

It became increasingly clear that the school board would remain deadlocked. As expected, the most vocal spokesman for a unified system was the one black member, the Reverend John Manley, pastor of the First Baptist Church and my colleague. But the votes were not there to carry the matter. Any hope of immediate integration would depend on electing new people to the board.

Binkley Church seized the opportunity to hasten the process by persuading a man in the congregation to declare himself a candidate. Fred Ellis had four daughters, one at every level of the school system. We promised that if he were elected we would relieve him of all responsibilities as a deacon, Sunday school teacher, and so on. We would consider his acceptance of this civic office as his church work for the next six years. He would be Binkley Church in the life of the world.

Fred Ellis was elected in 1961. He led the ticket with landslide support. Binkley members celebrated at his home where we watched election returns. Ellis's vote would now turn the tide on school integration. Indeed, at his very first official meeting, he made the motion that soon led to Chapel Hill becoming the first school district in North Carolina to activate a plan for total integration of the public schools voluntarily. All first-graders began their education in integrated classrooms in the fall of 1961.

Church people had played an influential role in moving the community toward compliance with the Supreme Court order, but a more difficult struggle just ahead would polarize the town and threaten violence in the streets.

Chapter 8

Crisis in the "Southern Part of Heaven"

They call Chapel Hill the "southern part of heaven," but in the winter of 1964 all hell broke loose. The crisis did not come upon us all at once. We eased into it. Steady progress in removing racial barriers had given the community a sense of relative well-being when compared to other places. Then the hope took hold that Chapel Hill could be the first town in the South to rid itself of even the last vestige of segregated service in public business establishments. So, protests persisted and escalated as racist holdouts dug in their heels. The liberal lighthouse community became all the more determined to tolerate no shadow of darkness at its base.

These were the years when the mood of the nation was quick to equate integration with liberalism and to make liberalism synonymous with communism. People across the state began to see the university as a radical, dissident den of activists. Critics were prone to label as suspicious any free-thinking person and to be extremely wary of any progressive idea that seemed threatening to the status quo. The John Birch Society and the House Un-American Activities Committee were doing their best to encourage this kind of reaction. This was also the trademark of a news commentator by the name of Jesse Helms from nearby Raleigh. He frequently editorialized about Chapel Hill on WRAL's evening news, thereby contributing to prejudice and suspicion against the town.

The hysteria of the extreme right increased in volume. Con-

servatives with a nationalistic fervor tried to equate Christianity
with the American way of life. Preachers discovered that their
congregations were much more likely to get upset over criticism
of their country than they were over theological heresy. National
loyalty began to take precedence over loyalty to the church as
people assumed that a major function of religion was to be the
foundation for democracy. Right-wing patriotism emerged as a
rival to the Christian faith as leaders tried to win the allegiance
of people by using religion as leverage.

Even in Chapel Hill this mentality proved intimidating. In
1963 the North Carolina legislature slapped a Speaker Ban Law
on all state institutions to render it illegal for any known communist to speak on state property. Chapel Hillians saw this action as punishment for the town's continuing crusade in the civil
rights struggle. Although the university refused to roll over and
play dead in response to the gag law, many professors on the
state payroll found it expedient to either keep silent or to weigh
any public statement carefully lest it be used against them later.
(The speaker ban legislation led to the formation of the North
Carolina American Civil Liberties Union, which held its initial
organizational meeting off campus in the local Presbyterian
church.) Watchdog Jesse Helms never missed an opportunity to
denigrate the university. Some years later, when the legislature
was urged to appropriate funding for a state zoo, Helms is credited with the quip, "All we need to do is to build a fence around
Chapel Hill."

I had been in touch with an organization known as the
Southern Conference Educational Fund. I was sympathetic with
all the printed materials sent to me and attended several of its
meetings. I knew the leadership had been put under a cloud by
the usual pejorative labels, but in so far as I could discern, what
others had called communistic was, in fact, representative of the
best of our American heritage.

In 1961 the board of the Fund asked if I would help arrange
a regional conference in Chapel Hill and serve as a sponsor. I
agreed, and secured the willingness of Vance Barron, minister
of the University Presbyterian Church, to work with me. He
bravely offered the downtown facilities of the church fellowship
hall for the event. The conference theme was "Freedom and the
First Amendment." Liberal leaders from central North Carolina

and beyond attended, and everyone involved considered the experience both timely and valuable.

This judgment was not shared, of course, by the detractors. A retired army colonel, serving as chairman of the Americanism Committee of the local American Legion post, fired off a salvo to the local press calling for a citizens' alert. He alleged that SCEF was conceived and financed by the Communist Party and that one of its primary goals was to stir up racial strife in the South. This type of accusation was not limited to this situation; it was used routinely. The colonel referred to me as that "minister who starred at a recent hearing of the Chapel Hill School Board when he verbally flagellated himself for having grown up in the segregated schools of South Carolina." Pink flyers were distributed that implied that all the sponsors of the conference were communist sympathizers.[1]

❦

The summer before the approaching civil rights crisis, there was a lull before the gathering storm. An unexpected opportunity came to Binkley Church that was exceedingly well timed. It provided a way to put to the test our professed racial convictions and to ferret out those last vestiges of prejudice that still remained. It would steel the congregation for what lay ahead. Although Binkley members were intellectually committed to social and economic integration, some folk had had little experience in personal, continuing friendships with Negroes.

In 1962 a telephone call came out of the blue from Union Theological Seminary in New York City informing us of a new program called Summer Interracial Ministry (SIM). It was a foundation-supported project that sought to place black seminarians in white congregations for a summer's internship and vice versa. A Negro student from Raleigh, North Carolina, wanted to participate. His name was James Forbes.

The intent of the call was to inquire whether Binkley Church would be willing to invite Forbes to Chapel Hill and finance his room and board. I took a deep breath and replied, "I hope so, but first I must clear it with our deacons." As I hung up the receiver, I felt apprehensive about what this opportunity would entail. I was by no means certain our church leaders would give their approval for Forbes to come.

After some initial hesitation, they did so, and with mounting enthusiasm. They began to see Forbes's coming as a means of upgrading our commitment to racial inclusiveness in the church. Up until now we had been willing to offer a ministry *to* Negroes; this would put us in position to receive a ministry *from* a Negro. Maintenance posed no problem. Forbes could live in the church house, and we believed his acceptance by the congregation would insure numerous invitations at mealtime.

Jim Forbes's coming was a God-send. He was a warm, personable human being with magnetic charisma. His first responsibility with us was to direct the Vacation Bible School. The children fell in love with him immediately, and their ready acceptance predisposed their parents to do the same. In June, Jim and I visited in homes of most of the membership so folks could feel each other out in a relationship that initially seemed strange to many.

On the first Sunday in July, Forbes and I stood behind the Communion table together to celebrate the Lord's Supper. By that time everyone seemed sufficiently comfortable with the situation for Forbes to share worship leadership with me. The atmosphere was charged with anticipation as the two of us took our places, black and white ministers side-by-side, to serve the bread and the cup. At the time it seemed a very daring thing to do. As the service proceeded, I experienced the miracle of reconciliation as seldom ever before, especially when we sang,

> Join hands then brothers of the faith,
> Whate're your race may be!
> Who serves my Father as a son
> Is surely kin to me.[2]

The tremendous impact of this service was evident not only from the expressions on the faces of the worshipers but also from their verbal comments afterwards. The experience had satisfied a deep hunger to rise above the racism that some only then were able to acknowledge.

Forbes's presence in our midst during the summer of 1962 forced all of us to understand vicariously the indignities suffered daily by Negroes everywhere. Binkley members had to think twice about the public places to which they could go in his company. Once Jim made a pastoral visit to a white mother in the maternity wing of the hospital where nurses were quick to steer him to the floor for black mothers instead.

By midsummer Forbes's acceptance was so complete that I confidently left him in charge of the congregation while I went away on vacation. At summer's end he led a weekend retreat at the beach that involved most of the membership. He enjoyed making jovial wagers about the likelihood of his returning home with the best sun tan. When the time came for Jim to leave Chapel Hill, everyone concurred that his coming had been the best thing that had ever happened to Binkley Church. In his own evaluation, he concluded: "One thing has become increasingly clear, and that is that real understanding requires genuine confrontation. . . . All my life I have heard white people say, 'We know our colored folks'; until this summer I thought I knew our white folks."

Subsequently, I submitted an article to the *Christian Century* that was published in January 1963, under the title "Interracial Ministry in the South." Readers across the country responded to me personally. A Southern Baptist missionary wrote from South America: "In the midst of the aberration and reactionaryism which seems to be dominating our convention at the moment, we take new hope when we hear of those who are unafraid— even in the face of great odds—to witness to Christianity in the modern world."

Later I had the privilege of performing Forbes's wedding when he became pastor of a Pentecostal church in Wilmington, North Carolina. He took an active role in that coastal city's civil rights struggle and was once jailed following a protest. Eventually he attracted national attention as a preacher and was invited to return to Union Theological Seminary as professor of homiletics. While there, he became one of the most sought-after pulpiteers in America, especially on college and university campuses.

At the University of North Carolina, Forbes's presence precipitated an unprecedented response from students to Binkley Church. On any given Sunday they made up more than half of the worshiping congregation. Clearly, the racial issue was ripe for further follow-up emphasis. That fall we invited Dr. Benjamin Mays, the distinguished black professor from Morehouse College in Atlanta, to deliver two lectures in Gerrard Hall. He was well known for his statesmanlike leadership and had written a splendid study guide called *Seeking to Be Christian in Race Relations* (New York: Friendship Press, 1957). Mays' visit was timely, for protests and picketing at segregated establishments in Chapel Hill were continuing intermittently. It was painful to admit the truth of the indictment made by our guest while at Chapel Hill: "Segregation could not exist if it had not been condoned by the churches. . . . For the most part ministers of the South have been the last ones to make any moves against segregation. . . . The churches have been more concerned with holding right biblical views than with effecting social change."

Mays further accused universities generally as being the second most conservative organizational entity in society, a judgment for which more evidence was forthcoming as efforts increased to desegregate Chapel Hill.

Imagine my chagrin when I discovered that Dr. Mays had been born in Greenwood County, South Carolina! No one there had ever told me that this famous gentleman grew up where I did. He had been without honor in his home country.

ఞ

The problem of an integrated campus adjacent to a partially integrated town was a festering sore point that edged the community toward racial conflict. By 1963 there were forty Negro students enrolled at the university, and at least a dozen of these worshiped regularly at Binkley Church. Several more became members. Our Student Affairs Committee was chaired by a newcomer to Chapel Hill named Dean Smith who was destined to become one of the most respected basketball coaches of the nation. (Several students who served with him have also made their mark on the national scene, including Denton Lotz, now the chief executive of the Baptist World Alliance, and David Price, who represents Chapel Hillians in Washington in the House of Representatives.)

As the racial climate became more highly charged, the Chapel Hill Ministerial Association, which was the professional organization of local clergy, became more assertive as the self-appointed monitor of all the goings-on. Some citizens began to complain about the persistent picketing, and businesses within the food service sector argued loudly that they had a constitutional right to serve in their restaurants whomever they pleased. Ironically, the word "freedom" became their rallying cry.

For months picketers had targeted the Colonial Drug Store, a business located not far from the Negro section of town and one that profited from many black customers. The manager, however, militantly resisted pressure to change his food counter policy. The point of contention was that the drug store had booths for white patrons that blacks were prohibited from using. Those who walked the picket line were black high school students, university students, professors, and preachers.

The most active white clergyman involved was Charles Jones, pastor of the Community Church. Charlie had been removed as pastor from the local University Presbyterian Church for heresy several years previously but had returned to Chapel Hill to be the first leader of the new Community Church congregation made up of many former Presbyterians. He was a pioneer social activist, widely known across the South. Many of his admirers were convinced that his ouster from the Presbyterian denomination had more to do with his liberal views on social issues than his unorthodox theology.

The protesters were commendably responsible. They attended training sessions at the First Baptist Church where participants were schooled in both the philosophy of Gandhi and the tactics of Martin Luther King, Jr. The temptation to reciprocate anger toward hostile hecklers was sometimes strong, especially for young teens, but no serious lapses in behavior were reported.

I took my turn on the picket line at Colonial Drug and felt the cold gaze of passers-by. Eventually, the manager attempted to reduce the tension by simply removing the booths and thereby making all his customers stand when served.

The worsening racial climate in the town led to the ministerial association becoming a close-knit support group. Nearly all ministers in Chapel Hill met together regularly with the same goal in view: to establish an inclusive community and to rid it completely of segregation. We felt some public statement from the Association might counter critics who imputed bad motives to those who picketed. The following excerpts are from a document signed by nearly every preacher in Chapel Hill, both black and white:

> We affirm our own conviction that what these protesters are seeking is only that to which they are justly and rightfully entitled as citizens. We deplore the fact that any group of our citizens is placed in the position of having to ask to be treated with dignity and respect. . . . We commend the leaders of these current protests for their dedication to the principles of non-violence. . . . We express our concern for those businessmen who may find themselves caught between their sense of right and their fear of economic suffering should they follow a course of serving all patrons on an equal basis. . . . We pledge our support to all business concerns which will follow the policy of equal treatment for all.

In the midst of this effort to influence public support of the picketing, the manager of nearby bowling lanes asked to be put on the association's agenda. He came to propose the organization of a church bowling league, but when he arrived at the

meeting and saw both white and Negro clergy together, he realized he had made a tactical error. He declined to make his pitch
because his establishment was open to whites only.

❧

I attended the Southern Baptist Convention in Kansas City
in May of 1963 when the racial conflict in Birmingham, Alabama, was the major focus of national and world news. More
than 2,500 persons had been jailed in Birmingham, including
Martin Luther King, Jr. The convention theme, "To Make Men
Free," could not have been more pertinent to what was happening, but as the closing session approached, it became apparent
that no one intended to take any stand on what was occurring
in that southern city. Ironically, most of those jailed there were
Baptists.

I could not keep silent. The former chaplain at the University of North Carolina, J.C. Herrin, helped me draft a resolution
calling for a more responsible use of our freedom in the elimina-
tion of discriminatory customs in the communities from which
we had come. "Too long we have laid waste our powers, dis-
sipated our resources, denied our common humanity, and violated our Christian witness," I said. The conclusion was a recommendation that inflamed many messengers, especially those
from Alabama, who felt unfairly maligned: a request that the
Southern Baptist Convention send a telegram "to our brothers in
jail in Birmingham" that would read, "You who are free in there,
pray for us who are in prison out here."

An Alabama pastor arose to oppose the resolution, and it
was buried in committee. Thus, the convention declined to
take any official action on the racial strife, but the motion was
noted in the lead story of the May 8, 1963, edition of the *Kansas City Star* and elsewhere in newspapers within Southern
Baptist territory.

❧

Meanwhile, things were heating up at home. A new group,
which called itself the Committee for Open Business, announced
plans to push for a municipal public accommodations law that
would end segregation in every remaining business holdout. The
idea received immediate endorsement from the one black alder-
man and the one white woman on the board. All the others
vacillated or insisted that the passing of such a local ordinance
was beyond their power to enact.

Various opinions were put forward. The Institute of Government in Chapel Hill, which studies North Carolina laws and their application, concluded that such local authority to enact the legislation did exist. Henry Brandis, dean of the law school, admonished protesters to cease their activities and to use instead the electoral system to replace those aldermen whose performance they judged to be unsatisfactory. He argued that the answer lay in the ballot box and not public demonstrations. The university as a whole kept silent except for the chancellor's reminder to the community that all the facilities of the university were integrated. Predictably, the *Chapel Hill Weekly*, which had consistently opposed the demonstrations, offered no support for the proposed ordinance.

Proponents of the public accommodations law pointed out that businesses were already subject to a wide array of restrictions and that the stand of the Businessmen for Freedom was ludicrous. Surely, human rights should have precedence over property rights in any case, they insisted. What could be more logical than the simple proposition that all members of the public should be given equal access to facilities open to the public?

Others observed that partial integration was a worse state of affairs than no integration at all since blacks were put in the position of always wondering where they would be welcomed. Obviously, merchants could not be forced to have goodwill, but it is precisely where goodwill is lacking that laws are necessary in any society. In a free society no private business is ever strictly private and no human being is ever excluded from membership in the general public.

As a preacher, I wearied in making repeated replies to those who pontificated, "You can't legislate morality." This is a half-truth at best. Clearly, one *can* legislate immorality! Segregation is the perfect example. Obviously, legislation can also create situations that make a moral response more likely. (In the effort to establish Prohibition, which the South led, southerners tried desperately to change custom by law.)

It is helpful to distinguish between the meaning of the terms desegregation and integration. Desegregation can remove barriers and provide more tolerant access between the races. Given such access, integration is more likely to follow. Integration, however, is more far-reaching in its impact than desegregation, for it implies a positive acceptance of others and a genuine interpersonal relationship. The physical proximity of blacks and whites may not eliminate prejudice, but prejudice probably will disappear more readily where people can freely intermingle than where people are legally separated.

The Committee for Open Business staged Chapel Hill's first sit-in, thus moving from orderly picketing to deliberately causing a disturbance. The Merchants Association office was the chosen place because of its symbolic significance and presumed influence over all local businesses. When the association's director, Joe Augustine, failed to persuade the protestors to leave, he called the police who distributed indictments for trespassing and arrested them all. Word of this new stage in Chapel Hill's worsening impasse led me to believe that it was imperative to address head on what was happening in Chapel Hill. The following is a portion of the sermon I preached the next Sunday:

> There remain [in Chapel Hill] at least fourteen business establishments that refuse to serve all people, and despite the moral persuasion of a large segment of our citizenry . . . these doors remain closed to Negro customers. . . . A man in business is required to operate his establishment within the framework of many laws. He is not free to pay his employees whatever he chooses . . . to hire children . . . to serve unhealthy food or to prepare it in a dirty kitchen. . . . His right of private property is contingent upon his acceptance of public responsibility. . . . If a man's business is in any way harming the public, then the public has a right to tell him how his business should be run. . . . [Some ask], "Is it not lawful for me to do what I want with mine own?". . . . The answer must be "No."

The civil rights movement peaked in the months ahead. In August of 1963, 250,000 citizens marched on Washington. Chapel Hill was well represented with busloads of people making the journey. We had raised funds to assist those who otherwise would not have been able to afford the fare.

Several weeks later, the tragic news of four young black girls killed by a bomb at Sunday school in a Birmingham church stunned the community. Pastor John Manley of First Baptist Church asked me to speak at a memorial service held there. The assignment proved painfully difficult, for I began to feel implicated in the crime simply because my skin was white. I said to the mourners assembled, "Those who murdered these children must have done so because they thought their deed would be approved and applauded. You and I must confess that we have lived in the kind of climate that would aid and abet that kind of thinking."

I continued to receive requests to go to other communities and speak on the racial issue. One Sunday evening I took my family with me when I went to preach in a black church in Greensboro. I was aghast when my young son innocently shouted to black teen-agers loitering on the church steps, "Hello, you old chocolate milk!" Of course, he meant it as an innocent greeting, but the response could have been hostile. Fortunately, it was rejoined with friendly laughter.

On another occasion, I was invited to speak to the Ministerial Association in Statesville. I was dismayed upon arrival to discover that the group was segregated. Not a single black was present. I chided them for this. Later, I received a telephone call from a black preacher in Statesville who had heard of my having spoken to his white colleagues. "Would you return to speak to the Negroes of Statesville?" he asked. I agreed and planned my return visit for a following Sunday afternoon. Late the night before, I had a call from Dr. O.L. Sherrill, the executive secretary of the General Baptist Convention (black) in Raleigh. "I hear you are going to Statesville," he said, "I'm going with you." I thanked him and protested the necessity of his accompanying me. To which he replied, "Brother Seymour, you need a bodyguard." He insisted, and I must say, I did feel more secure with him along. Sherrill looked like Mr. Clean; he was a giant of a man with a round, shining face. The tense racial climate in Statesville at the time could have provoked a confrontation, but no whites appeared at the gathering.

I had also become very much involved in the work of the North Carolina Council of Churches, first serving on the Human Relations Committee and then chairing the Social Service Commission. The Council had limited resources, but a recommendation from the Commission, inspired by the strong persuasion of Dr. Shelton Smith of Duke Divinity School, led to the employment of a full-time staff person to travel the state and work especially in the area of race relations.

Once the Council appointed me to be a fraternal messenger to seminary students from Massachusetts who had come down South to Williamston, North Carolina, to participate in protests, and as a result, had landed in jail. I was shocked upon arrival to see whites from the North walking down main street holding hands with blacks of the opposite sex. They had little idea how inflammatory this was to local residents and how such conduct

would likely negate any other gains achieved. It had been intended to symbolize the message of "hand in hand together," but
such interracial closeness between the sexes in the South suggested only the literal union of the races. I encouraged them to
be more discreet and sensitive to what local people might be
thinking lest they compromise their cause.

Then, at Thanksgiving in 1963, the devastating news of the
president's assassination in Dallas overwhelmed everyone. I had
supported John F. Kennedy enthusiastically and was convinced
he would do everything in his power to move the nation toward
civil rights legislation with teeth in it. News of his death made
me feel my moment in history had passed. He represented my
generation. He was my peer. He had given me high hopes that
the ideals of Camelot would remake America.

Our nation has never observed a more somber Thanksgiving. Any genuine blessing for which to be thankful stood out in
bold relief against the background of this unbelievable tragedy,
and so, I asked the following Sunday, "For what can we be
thankful as we reflect upon what has happened?" and answered:

> More than anything else . . . we . . . should be thankful for the
> redemptive nature of our God. . . . Our sense of loss is tempered
> by our belief in God's ability to meet us in whatever life brings and
> to call forth from even such an event as an assassination creative
> possibilities for good. . . . A specific redemptive consequence that
> may come from our president's death is a re-dedication to civil
> rights. . . . Surely, if the time were ever ripe to pass civil rights
> legislation, it is now. Somehow the death of this man makes it
> seem all the more imperative, for he will go down in history along
> side Abraham Lincoln as one who was courageously committed
> to liberating the racially oppressed in this land. . . . It just may be
> that his influence now is greater than ever before and that God
> will use it redemptively to further the crusade for liberty and
> justice for all.

December 1963 and January 1964 were the most difficult
times in the "southern part of heaven." Marches and sit-ins were
stepped up and more and more people were drawn to the front
lines of the struggle. At first, dozens were arrested, then hun-
dreds. A proliferation of groups emerged to seek ways to break
the impasse between opposing sides of the integration issue. The
mayor asked me to serve on a Mediating Committee with other
clergymen and I agreed. No one was willing to give an inch.
Aldermen refused to budge from their previous positions, and

the protesters promised to continue their disruptive demonstrations until a public accommodations law had passed.

The frustration level rose steadily. Everyone was hurting. Many were angry. Graham Creel, one of the key officers on the police force and an active member of Binkley Church, was supportive of the civil rights cause and found it very painful to be taking protestors to jail under the requirements of his job. He is reported to have been heard humming "We Shall Overcome" as he made his daily rounds.

Few questioned the courage or the sense of moral certitude that fueled the movement. Indeed, the significance of all this emanating from worship-like strategy sessions at First Baptist Church could not be overlooked. Even so, everyone wondered how much longer the impasse could continue without someone getting hurt and irreparable harm being done to the reputation of our community.

Increased pressure from outside Chapel Hill made things worse. James Farmer, the national Director of the Congress on Racial Equality (CORE), came to Chapel Hill and issued an ultimatum. He said he would mobilize the full strength of his organization against the community unless a public accommodations ordinance was passed forthwith. Word of his threat incensed Governor Terry Sanford who declared in no uncertain terms that he would not stand by and allow any outside group to put any town in North Carolina under siege. Now Chapel Hill was caught in the middle of a powerful deadlock, and control of the situation was in danger of getting beyond the ability of local officials.

The Ministerial Association responded by soliciting 1,800 persons to sign a petition in support of the public accommodations ordinance and published all the names in the *Chapel Hill Weekly* on January 12, 1964. A comparable attempt by the segregationists netted fewer than a hundred names. Mayor Sandy McClamrock appealed to the churches to state their positions on the matter publicly. Binkley deacons drafted a document declaring disapproval of segregation and discrimination, pledging "continuing effort and influence toward abolishing racial prejudice and injustice wherever they exist." The resolution was presented for adoption and was just nine votes shy of the unanimous approval of the congregation.

Civil disobedience escalated. Demonstrators were now lying down in the streets at major intersections and blocking the highway entrances into town. Local public support began to erode.

Residents felt unfairly inconvenienced, if not punished, for a situation that they reasoned was beyond their capacity to change. This new development in tactics was hotly debated, and many felt the demonstrators had gone too far. People accused the nonviolent participants of deliberately trying to incite a violent response from others.

The dean of the university law school chided the clergy for being accessories to the confusion by having created "scoff-law Christianity." When several professors from Duke Divinity School came over from Durham to stage a sit-in at a Chapel Hill restaurant, they justified their action on appeal to a higher law, but the whole effort began to look lawless to persons who had previously been sympathetic. They now called what was happening irresponsible.

Ugly incidents occurred. One of the worst one was when a restaurant owner's wife urinated on two demonstrators who had stretched out on the floor at the entrance to prevent customers from having access to the restaurant. At another business, protesters were doused with ammonia.

Things were getting out of hand, but the turmoil did not diminish until the protesters were summoned to court for the long hearings and trials and until the key leaders were sentenced to serve time behind bars. The presiding judge made no secret of his disdain for the tactics the protestors had used. He was a Baptist layman, and in a talk at a nearby church had said, "All this disturbance we have seen in the name of religion is a prostitution of religion."

Without interference from outside the community, which had accelerated the culminating crisis, Chapel Hill might have become the only town in the South to pass a municipal public accommodations law prior to the federal one. Instead, we waited for the national government to act. Those who disliked the ordinance could then blame Washington instead of town hall.

The demonstrators came up with one last dramatic gesture. Five young people, black and white together, staged a Holy Week fast on the post office lawn. From Palm Sunday to Easter morning, they stayed there day and night in full public view. They explained their witness to be in remembrance of the sufferings of Christ and also to draw a comparison between Pontius Pilate and the people of Chapel Hill who had failed to make a decision. They felt that Chapel Hill leaders had allowed a tragedy to happen that could have been prevented.

When President Johnson finally signed the new federal legislation guaranteeing equal access of all citizens to all public accommodations, Chapel Hill clergy took the lead to make sure everyone would comply. Coach Dean Smith agreed to team up with me and a black friend to integrate The Pines restaurant, which had one of the longest and loudest records of resistance. The Pines had also been the place where the university basketball team ate many of its meals. Thus, the coach seemed a perfect choice to usher in a new era. We were welcomed and seated and served as if no past racial exclusion had ever occurred. We could never have guessed then that in the very near future most of the players on the basketball team would be black!

Reports of this incident at The Pines involving Coach Smith have been embellished to apocryphal proportions in frequent subsequent recountings, much to Dean's embarrassment. Several years later, a feature article about Dean in *Sports Illustrated* (November 29, 1982) also included a photograph of the coach's pastor, as if the two of us had integrated the entire town, much to *my* embarrassment.

⁖

During this time of protracted crisis, I was blessed by the solid support of the people of Binkley Church. They understood the extra demands made upon me by the community, yet I knew I could never allow my local involvements to be all-consuming of my time. Pastoral responsibilities, church administration, and the ongoing agenda of the congregation could not be neglected even though members recognized these other activities to be the legitimate work of Christ's church. The privilege of a pastor's being active in the life of the world outside the congregation is intimately related to the pastor's being faithful to the day-to-day needs of people within the congregation. Indeed, the journey outward and the journey inward are mutually supportive. One can never be given up for the sake of the other even though there are times when each inevitably receives less attention that it deserves. With pressure pushing hard on both fronts, the promise of grace commensurate to one's need becomes a proven reality.

A growing frustration felt by Binkley members was the inconvenience of our temporary location on the university campus, although for six years this had served us exceedingly well. We were especially pleased by the response of students to our ministry which was, in large measure, made possible by our close proximity in Gerrard Hall. However, we now looked forward to being in a building of our own elsewhere.

We were hard-pressed to find money. In a sense we were in a Catch-22 situation for our margin of growth was largely of young people who had limited finances. Faced with this dilemma, we boldly requested a meeting with the missions committee of the Myers Park Baptist Church in Charlotte while Carlyle Marney was pastor. We made a strong case for the claim that any church in Chapel Hill belongs to the whole state since young people come to the university from everywhere in North Carolina. We also knew that Myers Park was sympathetic to the directions in which Binkley Church was moving in regard to both racial and ecumenical inclusiveness. "How much?" they asked. When we answered, "Twenty-five thousand dollars," they didn't bat an eye. Their gift enabled the church to make a down payment on a permanent home and to proceed with the long-delayed building project on the lot obtained through the Yates Baptist Association, the same association which had denied us membership.

One thing we learned during those long first years on campus in a borrowed facility is that a church is not bricks and mortar but people and spirit. Yet having had no visible building of our own in the community had been a handicap; many newcomers never knew we were there.

In October 1964, the congregation moved to the eastern edge of town with some apprehension. We feared we would cut ourselves off from students altogether and become a captive to suburban blandness and isolation, but God had something else in view. Soon we found ourselves in the middle of the new Chapel Hill in one of the most choice and coveted locations of our rapidly growing "village."

Chapter 9

Building an Inclusive Community

Despite mounting cynicism about American involvement in Vietnam, idealism about improving racial relationships here at home persisted. Now black and white children were attending school together, and Negro customers were seated and served in places previously closed to them. Clearly a new day had come to the South that would change it forever. The traditional understanding of the place of blacks in a predominantly white world was blurred beyond recognition. Psychologically, the boundary lines of the Old South would remain a factor for some time, for civil rights legislation failed to achieve dramatic reversals of personal attitudes overnight. Nevertheless, those who yearned for an inclusive society felt vindicated and confident of its coming.

Such was the mood of Binkley Church when the congregation occupied its new building on the 15–501 bypass in the fall of 1964. Optimism ran high. Jokes about the danger of being called "the By-pass Baptist Church" evoked little laughter. Even though students had been left behind on campus more than a mile away, and the majority of black Chapel Hillians were on the other side of town, the commitment to be a part of the community at large did not diminish with the move.

This commitment was symbolized by several nationally known guests who participated in the dedication of the new building. One of these was Dr. Samuel Proctor, the black preacher who had just completed a stint as deputy director of the

Peace Corps. Another was Dr. Edwin Tuller, the senior executive
of American Baptist Churches in the U.S.A., formerly the Northern Baptist Convention.

Tuller's visit coincided with the strong feeling of some Binkley members that the time had come for the congregation to
move beyond the confinement of Southern Baptist life to more
relevant relationships, transcending regional provincialism.
Surely Baptists in this country should no longer be separated a
hundred years after the Civil War.

Binkley began meeting with representatives of several dozen
churches from both conventions that belonged to a new organization called Baptist Unity. Further interest in seeking wider
relationships resulted from a study of a book, *Baptists North and
South* (Valley Forge: Judson Press), coauthored by Dr. Samuel
Hill (southern Baptist) and Dr. Robert E. Torbet (northern Baptist). Dr. Hill was then a professor in the Department of Religion
at the university and a Binkley member. Seeking to heal the
rupture caused by slavery a century before, both conventions
agreed to convene simultaneously for face-to-face fellowship at
Atlantic City in 1964 and to overlap their agendas for shared
programming.

It was there that the Baptist unity movement peaked. More
than three hundred clergy attended a banquet to hear Carlyle
Marney, pastor of the Myers Park Baptist Church in Charlotte.
Marney shrewdly observed that no Baptist bishops were present.
(It was he who coined the phrase "South of God.") This was a
grass roots crusade that had little chance of going anywhere.
Southern Baptists and American Baptists still viewed each other
with distorted and prejudicial impressions. Northerners tended
to see southerners as fundamentalists and racists, while Baptists
in Dixie accused Yankees of being too formal, liberal, and lacking in evangelical zeal.

At this same Atlantic City meeting, Southern Baptists turned
down a strongly worded recommendation of its Christian Life
Commission that commended churches that pledged to support
civil rights laws. Instead, by a secret vote, messengers approved
a motion that said that race relations are a matter for individual
churches. During the preceding debate, one minister from Alabama complained that any pronouncement from the Convention
"would destroy his efforts to keep Negroes out of his church." A
counterstatement in the report's preamble that did survive accused Southern Baptists of having been "a part of a culture
which has crippled the Negro and then blamed him for limping."

Actually, all kinds of Baptists are in both conventions. One primary difference I've seen, particularly in relation to the civil rights movement, is that Southern Baptist leadership typically tests to see which way the wind is blowing and then acts accordingly. American Baptist leaders, on the other hand, are more likely to set the pace and to steer constituents in more responsible directions. An illustration of this is the way American Baptists have been committed to the ecumenical movement and were charter members of the National Council of Churches while Southern Baptist leaders have consistently opposed any formal relationship to the larger inclusive church.

When invited to engage in a massive national pulpit exchange to celebrate the Baptist Jubilee Advance, Southern Baptists declined on the plea of limited interest. The fact is, the denominational leadership felt it would be risky to have all those Yankee preachers in southern pulpits even for one Sunday! Conversely, American Baptists had their own private fears about overtures toward unity, too. They knew that their much smaller denomination could be swallowed up by the Southern Baptist giant, never to be heard from again.

Though no mass movement to unite the two conventions ever materialized, it was still possible for a local congregation to transcend the longstanding division by becoming dually aligned. This permitted a church to belong to both bodies and to bear witness to the hope that someday Baptists North and South might be one. After lengthy deliberation, Binkley Church requested an American Baptist affiliation while retaining its Southern Baptist relationship. The two most compelling reasons for doing so were to avoid the provincialism so frequently characteristic of Southern Baptist life and to join a denomination more actively involved in social issues. Thus, the congregation now had access to the opportunities and obligations of both conventions.

Several neighboring Baptist churches saw our unifying move as a betrayal of loyalty to our southern roots. One correspondent judged, "This is okay for people who don't believe anything to begin with." Others saw it as it was intended: a symbolic step toward eventual reconciliation between Baptists northern and southern. Significantly, these two predominantly white bodies gave little or no thought to the eventual merging with the major Negro Baptist denominations as well.

In answer to the occasional question, What kind of Baptists are you? I replied, "We are Baptists in the best sense of

the word," for each Baptist congregation is free and autonomous. Each church can shape its own future in whatever direction the membership chooses. In actuality, however, many
congregations follow the course of least resistance and
become carbon copies of one other by adopting the denominational programming uncritically.

❧

I began to feel increasingly isolated within Southern Baptist
life. Once one gets the reputation of being a liberal, one is left out
in the cold. I was never extended an invitation to speak, preach,
or even pray at state Baptist conventions. The only place I was
ever asked to serve was on the Christian Life Committee where
our task was to write an annual report on the moral state of the
nation. The committee had no budget nor power to act. The
report was printed and distributed for reading as an academic
exercise, a kind of procedural ritual that was then promptly
forgotten.

The Southern Baptist Sunday School Board was extremely
cautious lest anybody think it pushed a social gospel agenda. A
furor erupted when someone noticed that black author James
Baldwin's "R" rated book *Another Country* was listed in the
bibliography of a publication for young people. The publisher
apologized profusely for failure to edit it out, and all forty-
nine Baptist bookstores across the South sent out disclaimers
to make certain their constituents understood that the book
had no official sanction.

Later, a similar incident occurred that was reminiscent of
the 1958 recall of the study book by the Home Mission Board.
A critical response to a photograph on the cover of a youth
publication, which showed two white teen-age girls talking to a
black boy, led to a recalling of 160,000 copies.

In general, Southern Baptist churches were more likely to
mirror culture than to speak to it. Following the assassination of
John Kennedy, the Convention saw nothing inappropriate in
holding its annual meeting in Dallas where W.A. Criswell, the
much publicized pastor of the First Baptist Church, repeatedly
decried integration as idiotic. This was the same man who had
done his best to prejudice Baptists against voting for the Roman
Catholic president.

Obviously, the projection of this kind of image did not play
well in a university town. Persons from other denominations
who expressed interest in becoming members of Binkley Church

hesitated to be known as Baptists. It was easier to project a new image by letting it be known that we were affiliated with American Baptists, too.

ℬ

Our new building opened up new opportunities for ministry from the day it was occupied. The facility consisted of a large fellowship hall (which doubled as an interim sanctuary), office space, and classrooms for Sunday school. Having ascertained a shortage of places for kindergarten-age children in our growing community (before kindergartens became a part of the public school system), we decided to get maximum use of the education space by establishing a weekday program. From the outset, a stated policy made it clear that the kindergarten would be interracial and that a percentage of placement slots would be set aside for families who could not afford to pay.

Implementation of this racially inclusive policy proved almost impossible. Naively we had assumed that our white middle-class lifestyle had its black counterpart. We soon learned that black parents required all-day care for their children, not half-day care. The nonworking black mother who could pick up her child at noon was almost nonexistent. As a result, scholarships routinely went to international student couples, including several from Africa. Not until 1970, when our nursery became a daycare center, were we successful in including many black children.

Chapel Hill had few public buildings with adequate parking. Our church was a notable exception. We were besieged by numerous groups who requested the use of our facility as a regular meeting place. Whenever possible, we welcomed them. People began to think of our building as a community center, for it housed a wide range of activities— everything from Boy and Girl Scouts to Alcoholics Anonymous, to the League of Women Voters, to the Sierra Club, eventually providing headquarters for over fifty service, civic, and special-interest groups. One of the few organizations denied access was the new Mormon congregation, due to its then discriminatory policies toward both blacks and females.

ℬ

In the sixties we suddenly discovered widespread poverty in our land of opportunity, and our president declared war against it. Lyndon Johnson launched an array of innovative programs aimed at improving education and the employability of poor people. In the South, the majority of the deprived were blacks. No longer locked in legal separation, they were theoretically now free to move into the mainstream of America, even in Dixie. But despite the demise of segregation, the cycle of poverty threatened to keep many blacks prisoners to a marginal existence.

Some black churches had been engaged in programs to help their members economically for a long time. A few congregations organized credit unions so that those who needed to borrow could have access to loans that may not have been granted by local banks. Southern banking institutions were generally hard-nosed about collateral; their policies in loaning money were illustrative of that old principle that "those that has, gets."

I recall a visit to the black First Baptist Church in Winston-Salem where, much to my amazement, I saw large blackboards lining the walls of the vestibule on which were written the names of all the members and a weekly public record of their Sunday-by-Sunday offerings. "How do you get away with this?" I asked the pastor. Mr. Hedgley replied, "Oh, you don't understand, Brother Seymour. We post this information so that we can see who needs help. If we notice that someone has failed to give anything to the church for several months running, we seek them out to see if they need assistance from us!"

Ironically, many of the same prejudices held against poor people are identical to those leveled against blacks. They are lazy. They are dirty. They are happy as they are. They are undeserving. Such judgments are deep-seated in southern culture and are readily applied to both black people and poor people alike. When the poor people happen to be black, the hope of a rational approach toward solving their problems becomes more difficult because of the stubborn legacy of prejudice.

The churches of Chapel Hill recognized local poverty before the federal government did. A group of church women discovered some appalling conditions even within the town limits. They found black families living in hovels unfit for human habitation. Several houses even had dirt floors with no electricity or plumbing. The women made Band-Aid responses as best they could but quickly concluded that more substantial help was required, so they approached the Ministerial Association with a report of their findings and urged the forming of a social service agency as an arm of the faith community. This marked the beginning in 1963 of what became the Inter-Faith Council (IFC). Serving as the first president for seven years, I saw the Council begin in an inauspicious way and gradually expand in its effectiveness to become the most respected social service organization in Chapel Hill.

Initial projects of the Council aimed at meeting simply the basic human needs. Volunteers made regular distributions of food to nearly a hundred families by acting as the delivery system for the commodities made available through the United States Department of Agriculture. The Council also collected clothing and cast-off furniture to distribute to the poor. Sensitive to the danger of paternalism, the Council recruited several blacks to serve as members of the board of directors. The clothing center became a cooperative that was administered by the same people who benefited from its use.

The IFC assumed an advocacy role to seek justice for persons who were victims of practices over which they had no control. For example, we discovered that the standard policy of the university-owned utilities was to cut off customers' water supply if they failed to pay their light bill on time. Increasingly, underprivileged people turned to the Inter-Faith Council in every occasion of crisis, and it became exceedingly difficult to decide where the limited financial resources could be put to most effective use.

Another major activity for volunteer involvement was tutorials. Now that blacks and whites were competing with one another in the same classroom, many black children who had come from an inferior educational experience needed compensatory help. Others simply needed a quiet, supervised place to study. Scores of adults and university students gave countless hours to this never-ending task every weekday evening. When the federal government's Head Start program first got under way in the summer of 1965, many of these same volunteers made door-to-door visits all over the area to seek out those young children who would begin first grade in the fall and would profit from such supplementary preparation prior to beginning public school.

The Council came up with the idea of a camping experience for youngsters from low-income families during the summer months. We rented a large empty rural barn surrounded by pasture and asked the Welfare Department to put us in touch with boys and girls who might most benefit from an enrichment program. Church members offset the cost by offering scholarships. The success of the project caught the attention of another local group seeking to organize a YMCA. This group accepted the challenge of continuing a summer camp, and it is still in operation.

Early in its life, the Inter-Faith Council developed a spin-off policy. After responding to some particular community need through the coordinated work of volunteers, it then welcomes the opportunity to put the project in someone else's hands, as was done with the summer camp. Another illustration of this policy is the origin of the Orange County Department on Aging which got its start through the Council's expanding ministry to older people. Repeatedly, the Inter-Faith Council has been a catalyst in creating a broad spectrum of services in the community.

🕉

North Carolina preceded the federal government with a state-supported poverty program similar to the national VISTA (Volunteers in Service to America) program. It was called the North Carolina Fund and recruited college students into a kind of domestic peace corps to work with poor people across the state. The Inter-Faith Council contracted with the governor's office for a team of young people to spend a summer in several pockets of poverty in black neighborhoods in Chapel Hill.

These young people arrived full of idealism, but some of their initial enthusiasm soured quickly. They had received limited orientation about what to expect and were surprised when some of the children from low-income black families showed up on the playground looking clean and prosperous, causing the volunteers to wonder if the boys and girls were truly needy. They were also troubled by the discovery that some of them came from homes where there were television sets. Cynical complaints from the volunteers about such findings ballooned into a crisis with the threat of several team members resigning.

Fortunately, the situation was salvaged by the wisdom of Geraldine Gourley, a professor from the School of Public Health and a member of the IFC Board. She explained to the young people that it was relatively easy in America for anyone to appear well dressed because of the availability of inexpensive and used clothing. When you meet people on the street, it is impossible to judge who is poor and who is prosperous. Furthermore, black mothers who live in poverty often make an extra effort to dress their children in ways to disguise their deprivation.

As for television, should the poor be denied such pleasure? People who are condemned to live in drab and dilapidated housing that landlords refuse to repair need some way to escape their shabby surroundings. This same explanation defuses critics of southern blacks for driving nice cars. Often a poor person who has no hope of ever owning a decent house purchases a fine automobile as a kind of substitute home on wheels.

To counteract such misunderstandings of the culture of poverty, I preached a series of sermons intended to inform and clarify the issues. Among other things I said that much in our attitude toward the poor adds up to continuing suspicion that they are somehow undeserving. There is a persistent tendency to assume that if a man is poor, something must be wrong with him. The sermon continued,

> We seldom assume that something is wrong with the system. We would like to believe that it is our initiative and hard work that has put us where we are, not the good fortune of our birth and the good breaks that have come to us along the way. To raise any question about the system would contribute to our sense of insecurity. We might begin to wonder how deserving *we* are, and we would not want to contemplate this. As God has been merciful to us, so are we called to be merciful to each other. The Scripture doesn't say, "Be merciful only to those who are deserving." No, it simply says, "sees his brother in need"—any brother. The fact of need is all you need to know.

It is surely significant that in the closing months of Martin Luther King, Jr.'s prophetic career, he moved beyond his concern about racism to call attention to poverty. His crusade to end segregation led to a heightened awareness of de facto segregation wherever people are economically deprived. Who can gauge where King might have gone with this? He was in Memphis siding with striking garbage collectors when the assassin's bullet struck. When his successor, Ralph Abernathy, came through Chapel Hill with a contingent of protesters on the Poor Peoples' March on Washington, Binkley Church opened its building to them. They were invited to cook in the church kitchen and bed down on the fellowship hall floor. The movement to organize the poor, however, never fully materialized after King's death.

The timing of King's death could not have been more symbolic. During Holy Week of 1968, he became a Christ figure. His unflinching courage was like that of Jesus who steadfastly set his face toward Jerusalem. His death at the hands of his enemies made us feel that King had died for our sins. All at once, the passion narrative became disturbingly contemporary, but the anguish over King's murder gradually gave rise to the cautious hope that redemption and resurrection might yet change the world.

❧

Because Binkley Church had been founded with the dream of becoming a genuinely interracial fellowship, we were frustrated by our failure to attract more black members. Never were there more than five or six black families in the congregation at any given time. This made it seem all the more imperative to seek other ways to make visible our belief in the one body of Christ. Therefore, when our white secretary resigned, we intentionally sought a black replacement. We knew her central role in the day-to-day life of the church would send a clear message to anyone who entered the office. We continued to provide opportunities for black students from nearby Duke Divinity School to serve as interns and assigned to them regular liturgical responsibilities to keep them visible in Sunday worship. Also, in the years immediately after King's death, the church joined others in remembering his birthday by closing the office, in the hope that the practice would spread.

King's martyrdom awakened many southerners to the urgency of overcoming the legacy of racism. For too long southerners had looked the other way and pretended all was well where oppression was the norm. For years the southern church had exported its finest youth to brave distance, disease, and tropical heat and jungle, while ignoring acute human needs in our own backyards.

In her book *Killers of the Dream*, Lillian Smith includes an excerpt from a letter written by a young southern girl who had just been appointed to go to Africa by the Southern Baptist Foreign Mission Board: "I wanted to stay in the South . . . that is what I really wanted to do. But there was mother . . . you know how disgraced she would have felt had I stayed and helped there. But she is proud of me now, going off to Africa as a missionary. . . . I am the only one ashamed. Tonight I feel like a coward for I know I am needed here."[1]

At last the proud hypocrisy of the past was being exposed for what it was, and though some still wanted desperately to cling to the mythology of a culture in which all is sweetness and light, this was no longer possible. The searchlights of the national press left few places to hide. In this new context, the voice of the church began to insist that missions begin at home. In light of that, the experience the Binkley congregation had while assessing its mission giving was typical of an agonizing reappraisal of priorities that occurred in a few places across the South. How could the church justify channeling so much of its benevolent giving elsewhere when there were such desperate situations nearby? It seemed inconsistent to appeal for sacrificial funding for the other side of the world and to do nothing about equally urgent needs on the other side of town. Unlike the biblical character Dives, who probably also supported many diverse and good causes, we could no longer be callous to the suffering beggar who slept at our doorstep.

We proposed the launching of a major outreach project in Chapel Hill to be supported solely by Binkley Church. If missions begin at home, what should our mission be? We asked the finance committee to include in the new budget an undesignated line item of $5,000 for a new local service project. Then we appointed four teams of Binkley members to act as separate task forces to scout out the community to seek places where the investment of a little money might make a big difference. On consecutive Sunday evenings, each of the teams reported back to the congregation and competed with one another in trying to persuade the church to fund the project it recommended. A lot of information about the town was amassed in the process, and, eventually, the three remaining proposals left on the drawing board were activated by others.

The project that fired the imagination of the church and won the majority vote of the congregation was to establish a satellite community center in a well-defined low-income neighborhood in the black ghetto. This would be a place where a broad range of activities could occur, and Binkley members would be directly involved as volunteers as well as contributors of money for the ongoing cost.

The task force that proposed this winning project had also discovered a civic need to dismantle an old house in downtown Chapel Hill which, up until then, had served as the town's public library. The property was about to be put to other use. We were challenged to do a demolition job in exchange for the gift of three small buildings to the rear of the large house, all of which could be moved and become community centers in other locations. This offer generated considerable enthusiasm, not only for what Binkley Church could do with one of the houses but also for the hope of challenging other congregations to start something similar with the remaining two buildings.

Then we hit a snag. A surge of growth in Binkley's membership had pushed our Sunday school space to the limit. Already we were renting a nearby dance studio for two adult classes, and now the children's rooms were overflowing. Some responsible leaders insisted that the time had come to add more rooms to the education wing and questioned the wisdom of establishing a community center when the crunch for space in our own building was so pressing. Others felt the mission project should be top priority regardless. Members pulled in both directions. Finally, in full awareness of the magnitude of the challenge, and after lengthy debate, the church voted to do both simultaneously. Dollars could be designated for either the building project or the missions project, depending upon where the donor judged the priority claim to be.

In the weeks and months that followed, Binkley members attacked the old house with a vengeance. Persons who had had little previous experience in wielding a hammer delighted in banging away at walls and beams. The task proved formidable. In due time, however, everything was cleared away, and the buildings destined to become community centers were professionally moved at considerable expense.

The Carr Court Community Center opened in May of 1968. The new municipal Office of Economic Opportunity agreed to accept the center as part of its Community Action Program (CAP). This government agency was the local manifestation of President Johnson's War on Poverty which was intended to make America "The Great Society."

To reach Carr Court, one had to follow a crumbling blacktop road behind a service station, cross rusty railway tracks, and pass an abandoned car. Beyond a weedy open space sat Carr Court, the only house on the shabby-looking street that had a basketball backboard in the front yard. At the time, approximately forty black families lived in the immediate area. There were more than a hundred children. People of all ages were drawn to the Center, first out of curiosity, but soon to participate in a wide range of activities, both educational and recreational.

The playground was supervised after school each day. Inside the house, Binkley women taught crafts, sewing classes, and personal grooming. Tutorial help in homework for school age children was always available. Instruction in art gave young people a chance to express themselves creatively. Coach Dean Smith arranged basketball clinics. During the summer, lunch was served to a multitude of children, and field trips took them to places of special interest within a day's travel distance from home. The majority of Binkley members became involved in the center in one way or another, and despite inevitable frustrations, the Carr Court Community Center thrived for six years.

Growth of the university student body led to the closing of campus swimming pools to local citizens who for many years had enjoyed access to them. Everyone not connected to UNC was now left without a place to swim except, ironically, the black population. Several years before, the town had constructed a pool near the center of the black community on Roberson Street. Although it was supervised by the Chapel Hill Department of Recreation and theoretically open to everyone, white persons seldom swam there. Most felt unwelcome to use the facility.

Almost overnight, several new pools were built in white suburbs. Without thought of the racial issue, my wife and I bought a membership in the Exchange Club pool so that our children could continue their water sports in the summertime. Much to our dismay, we later learned that a confidential policy statement governing the use of the pool specifically stated that memberships would not be sold to Negroes. We withdrew immediately.

Another pool was constructed near Binkley Church at Ridgefield for the use of families in the surrounding neighborhood. A Quaker couple who lived within sight of the pool had adopted a large number of children of various racial origins, including one child who was black. When they applied for membership at the nearby pool, their application was denied. The official explanation given was that the family had too many children!

Reports of what was said in a board meeting for the management of this same pool circulated in the community. Apparently a serious discussion concerned the propriety of a black maid taking a white child entrusted to her care to swim. Would this be permitted? If so, would the black maid be permitted to jump into the water to rescue the child in an emergency?

In the wake of such developments, I once again made an appeal from the pulpit for a conscious effort against racism, particularly racism in its new, more subtle forms. I further challenged my listeners never to assume the absence of racism but to ask questions of every group to which they belonged and of every place they entered and to withdraw from any organization or facility that refused to admit our Negro brothers and sisters.

University athletic programs set a better example. Dean Smith discussed with me the possibility of recruiting black basketball players, and of course I encouraged him to do so. It is hard to believe there were no blacks on the team until as late as 1967 when Charles Scott broke the color barrier and became the campus hero.

The same change was beginning to occur on the football field. A favorite joke of the time told of the alumni who could be heard shouting from the stands in the stadium, "Look at our colored boy tackle their nigger!" Even this could be cited as evidence of a new South emerging.

✿

These years of unrelieved pressure and protest were taking their toll. I welcomed the offer of our diaconate to take a summer leave for personal renewal. Pearl and I decided this would be an ideal time to go to Europe, now that our children were old enough to profit from the experience. A physician in the congregation became aware of our plans and asked if we would do him the favor of picking up a new Mercedes in Stuttgart and drive it around Europe so he could then import it as a used car. We readily agreed. Although we enjoyed touring the Continent in style, our fine automobile created understandable confusion when we pulled up at budget hotels!

After six weeks of sightseeing, my family flew home from Paris while I remained to make a visit to Russia alone. I had a strong desire to see to what extent I had been susceptible to U.S. government propaganda. In making travel arrangements, I was amused to discover Madison Avenue-like categories offered to American tourists in the Soviet Union: first class, deluxe, and super-deluxe! I opted for the middle one and was cared for very well. My Russian vocabulary consisted of only four words: "yes," "no," "please," and "men's room." Fortunately, I was blessed by excellent guides who spoke perfect English, even with an American accent.

Russia seemed every bit as gray and regimented as I had been led to believe. Sadly, the United States did not look much better from their perspective. That was the summer when race riots occurred in nearly every major American city, and *Pravda* never failed to put on the front page photographs of policemen with billy sticks chasing black people off the streets. No wonder

Russians thought their country was a paradise when compared to capitalistic oppression! I recalled Robert Burns's couplet, which I had learned to say in Scotland:

> O wad some Power the giftie gie us,
> To see ourselves as ithers see us.

A high point of my visit to Russia was attending the Sunday morning worship service at a large Baptist church in Moscow where I was warmly received. The congregation was overflowing with every seat filled and people standing. I wondered how people there might feel if the situation had been reversed—if they were visitors in my segregated home church and told that blacks were not welcome to worship with whites in South Carolina.

Chapter 10

Politics in the Church

At the height of my career as a clergyman, the either/or prediction of my high school yearbook became both/and. I became increasingly involved in politics. The vocations of the preacher and the politician are not far apart. Indeed, they are at times synonymous. Every politician needs a pulpit, and every preacher must be politic.

For the most part, Baptists are reticent to become political activists. They see the church as a place of refuge from the rough-and-tumble of life, and when they are warned from the pulpit about the danger of becoming too worldly, the laity often translates this to mean that the church is interested in spiritual things only. This perception lends weight to the popular dictum that religion and politics don't mix.

The case against political activism also rests upon a false understanding of the separation of church and state. More than any other denomination, Baptists claim credit for the incorporation of this founding principle in America's constitution. A Baptist preacher, John Leland, bent the ear of James Madison, who, in turn, persuaded other founding fathers to reject the concept of an established church. The intent of this separation was to insure freedom of the church from interference by the state. It also was meant to permit religious leaders to make prophetic judgments about government policy without fear of reprisals. Lamentably, many Baptists now think separation mandates an abdication of political involvement altogether. They get upset when their preacher speaks out on a political issue, for they think separation means that these two spheres of influence should be sharply distinguished and kept in different compartments.

The major exception to this prevailing perception is when a matter of personal morality becomes a political issue. For example, Baptists wage an unrelenting crusade against alcohol and seldom hesitate to instruct members of the flock to vote against its availability. In fact, the alcohol issue has so dominated Southern Baptist mentality that many will vote for candidates who stand for racism, imperialism, and fiscal insanity so long as they can stand without staggering! There has been little acceptance of the claim that every political matter has a moral dimension, whether it be about health, taxes, highways, education, or something else. Baptists have been slow to understand that God is not primarily interested in religion but is concerned about everything that happens in the world.

Obviously, religion and politics *do* mix. In a democracy, if citizens are to be responsible, the two must mix. We are simultaneously religious and political beings. How one votes inevitably reflects one's convictions. We cannot leave our beliefs outside the ballot booth. When Jesus said, "Render therefore unto Caesar the things which are Caesar's; and unto God the things that are God's" (Matthew 22:21), he surely meant that we are to be responsible in both areas.

Only once was I reprimanded for being too pointed in making a political judgement from the pulpit—when George Wallace ran for president. I abhorred the very thought of any Christian voting for this man. How could anyone who understands what America is all about consider a self-proclaimed racist as a serious contender for our highest office? I said,

> We must say a firm no to George Wallace and all that he represents. . . . The real George Wallace was speaking when he said in 1964 as governor of Alabama, "I'm gonna make race the basis of politics in this state and in this country." . . . He is a symptom of a serious national illness that will not be cured if we look away and pretend it does not exist. The Wallace movement is an evil phenomenon; he is not fit to be president of the United States.

Parishioners who objected to my forthrightness in calling Wallace by name had no intention of voting for him. They just thought I had violated my prerogative as a Baptist preacher by presuming to instruct voters in how to exercise their franchise.

❧

My more direct political involvement in Chapel Hill was precipitated by a project of the Inter-Faith Council. In its beginning years, the Council had directed all of its resources toward meeting emergency human needs. It assisted persons who fell between the cracks of social welfare legislation. Now an attempt was being made to remove some of the root causes of recurring problems by engaging in preventative actions.

A major need in the town, especially for black citizens, was better housing. As a nonprofit agency, the Council learned it could qualify to sponsor federally funded housing for low-income families. We retained a consultant to negotiate the red tape, and after repeated delays, eventually constructed seventy-eight apartment units.

As expected, the primary roadblock to the project was locating property. We viewed the site choice as an opportunity to disperse the black population and found a possible acreage in a buffer zone between a commercial district and a residential white neighborhood. Resistance surfaced overnight. Even though professors from the University Department of City Planning concurred that the location chosen was in line with proper zoning codes, the people who lived close by raised loud and angry objections. The racist fear that property values would decline was their rallying cry. As president of the Inter-Faith Council, I became the target of considerable criticism. Lake Forest homeowners judged me to be insensitive to their fear of impending financial loss.

A prolonged struggle began when the Council asked the town board to rezone the property so we could use it. People packed the public hearing. Feelings ran high. As I left one such meeting, a man hissed and shouted, "Why don't you do us a favor and leave Chapel Hill?"

It became increasingly apparent that the only hope of breaking the impasse was to elect new representation. We were sure many fair-minded citizens were behind the project. Everyone seemed to understand the desperate need for additional domiciles for the service-related segment of the population. As Chapel Hill grew, more and more families at the lower end of the economic ladder found it difficult to live in such an affluent place. Some were forced to settle in neighboring towns and be bused back and forth to work. But even if blacks had had the money, there would have been little chance of escaping the ghetto to buy a place elsewhere, for realtors were resistant to selling homes to blacks in white areas. Open housing was not yet legally enforceable.

Enter Howard Lee, candidate for mayor. Lee had brought his family to Chapel Hill so he could get a degree in social work. They lived in university housing where there was no discrimination. Shortly after arriving, Howard and his wife, Lillian, joined Binkley Church. Lee was an outstanding young man. He was positive in attitude, personable, and intelligent. His potential for leadership was even more impressive in the light of his family origin, for he is the son of a Georgia sharecropper. And Howard Lee is black.

After completing his university degree, Howard accepted employment in nearby Durham but decided to make Chapel Hill his home. He took steps to purchase a house in a middle-class white suburb, a first for Chapel Hill. The realtor was under strong pressure to deny the sale; he was convinced his whole development would slide into devaluation if a black family moved in. Anonymous telephone calls to the Lees became so threatening that Lillian summoned her pastor for reassurance. Hatred in all its ugliness had so upset her as to make them question the safety of going ahead with their purchase. Later, the telephone company traced these venomous calls to the realtor's office! His secretary had made them. Once the Lees were settled, the neighbors accepted them readily, assisted by a Binkley family nearby who invited everyone in to meet them.

Lee was still relatively unknown in Chapel Hill when Rebecca Clark, a leader among local blacks, planted the seed that he should consider running for mayor. It took little persuasion to get him to file. Even though potential supporters thought he had little or no chance of winning, we encouraged his candidacy. At least he would offer the electorate a clear choice and give liberals a rallying point. Lee pledged unapologetic support of the INCHUCO (Inter-Church Council) Housing project right from the start.

Meet-the-candidate coffees blanketed the town. People who attended solely to satisfy their curiosity about this black man who had the audacity to run for mayor in even this liberal (by southern standards) community usually left convinced he could do the job. Howard had a winsome persuasiveness that proved irresistible to everyone he met. He quickly gained the following

of many assertive whites. Funding the campaign proved no problem. Enthusiasm mounted, but as the election approached, even
his supporters realized that Lee's bid for office in a predominantly white southern town was at best a long shot.

A high point in the campaign was a political rally and picnic
staged on the spacious lawn of the Baptist Campus Ministry
house. Contrary to all precedents, the chaplain, Jack Halsell
(also a member of Binkley Church) agreed to rent this choice
central place to Citizens for Howard Lee. The annual BSU report
evaluated the occasion as follows:

> This turned out to be a highly significant event to encourage per-
> sonal contact between various fragments of our town and cam-
> pus—black and white, students and professors, town and gown,
> rich and poor. Over a thousand attended. That it was on the
> grounds of the Baptist Student Center was a testimony to our
> concern for the quality of life of our community. As a learning
> experience for students, it was a way of showing the interest
> Christians should have in the political order.

Howard's opponents kept waiting for him to stub his toe, but
he never did. He skillfully mended fences among white constituents and renewed the hope of blacks who were about to lose faith
in the political system.

Howard Lee was elected! As tabulations came in from precinct after precinct, the level of elation soared. Incredibly, Howard garnered 55 percent of the votes, most of which had been
cast by whites. He was the first nonwhite in the South to be put
in office in a municipality where blacks were in a minority.

That 1969 election night remains a radiant memory. Supporters had been invited to a victory celebration at St. Joseph's
Christian Methodist Episcopal Church, a black congregation on
Rosemary Street. The sanctuary was filled, and people were
standing both inside and out. Clapping and singing were deafen-
ing and continued late into the evening. Nobody wanted to go
home. This black church was mixing politics and religion without apology, and we celebrated as if a miracle had occurred.
Indeed, it had.

How proud I was to be known as the mayor's pastor! The
effect of Lee's election was to open up the traditionally elite
centers of power to people who had always felt excluded. The
politics of inclusion was now the new order of the day. Blacks
were appointed to places of responsibility at every level of local
government. All the municipal boards brought blacks and whites

together, the privileged and the less privileged, as working partners. Those who had so recently charged that Chapel Hill's liberal image was a fraud were effectively silenced.

Shortly after Howard's election, the Southern Christian Leadership Conference sent a certificate to Binkley Church that bore a picture of Martin Luther King, Jr., and had the following inscription over Ralph Abernathy's signature: "In grateful recognition of your unselfish support in assisting us in the continuing struggle to bring about an end to racism, poverty, and war. With your unshakable faith we cannot help but attain that new day when all people can live together in peace, in justice, and in love."

Howard ignored the myth that Chapel Hill was a village. He governed it as a rapidly growing town. One major achievement was persuading the community to establish a public transit system. He took steps to insure the preservation of open space before commercial development seized everything. In short, Lee inaugurated a period of political activism that continues to this day.

The racial issue still lurked in the background. White racists resented the mayor's authority and predicted ineptness; black racists accused him of selling out to white folks. Lee's greatest test came in dealing with university cafeteria workers on strike, most of whom were black. He successfully walked the tightrope of gaining the respect of university officials while securing fairness for the exploited employees. The community also gave the mayor high marks for the way he directed law enforcement officers in their response to frequent public demonstrations by persons who opposed the war in Vietnam.

The Inter-Faith Council approached Mayor Lee about requesting the assistance of a VISTA team to work in Chapel Hill. VISTA was the federal program that assigned volunteers to assist in deprived communities of the nation. Word of the request shocked the town. Few wanted to admit that conditions in the "southern part of heaven" warranted such outside help, but Howard refused to be dissuaded and put the weight of his office behind our request. Soon twelve able young people arrived to work with Chapel Hill's poor. Binkley's Carr Court Center played an important role in the success of this undertaking, for its resident director, Roger Hardister, was tapped by the town to supervise the whole VISTA program.

Lee, keeping his campaign promise, pushed public housing. The INCHUCO project had elicited a long waiting list of persons who needed better places to live. At this time other federal programs were accessible to the town with money available only for the asking. As had been the case with the church-sponsored project, civic planners desired to make possible residential addresses for blacks in all parts of Chapel Hill. The first site selected was a stone's throw from Binkley Church. Soon forty-four black families would be our neighbors in the Ridgefield Apartments, and Binkley Memorial would be the closest congregation.

The usual fears were expressed by white homeowners whose backyard property lines abutted the housing project. These were lower-middle-class homes, not in the same category as the more expensive homes in Lake Forest where people had protested INCHUCO. In both cases, however, their fears of falling property values proved unfounded. Not a single house in either neighborhood has been sold for a lower price than its original purchase cost.

Binkley deacons discussed how to reach out to their new neighbors. The most obvious suggestion was carried out soon after the tenants moved in; they teamed up two-by-two and visited every household.

I am not sure anything Binkley members might have said would have resulted in the new Ridgefield residents attending Binkley Church. We now faced a different barrier, one more readily accounted for by class than by race. These were people of limited means. They were blue-collar folk. Some were welfare recipients and had no advanced education; whereas, at Binkley, the congregation was made up mainly of professional people with graduate degrees.

We were experiencing a basic flaw of Protestantism: the difficulty of maintaining a heterogeneous congregation. The sermon is a prominent part of worship and is usually tailored to the educational level and culture of the majority of the congregation. This, coupled with the fact that there are frequent social gatherings of the congregation, causes persons not of similar background to feel uncomfortable and out of place. Indeed, Binkley Church never succeeded in its attempt to include all social classes. The black people who were attracted to the congregation were relatively well off and well educated. In short, they were like the white majority.

We looked for other ways to be a good neighbor. Completion of the Ridgefield housing coincided with the construction of a new shopping mall directly across the highway from the project and adjacent to the church. This afforded a ready-made opportunity to seek employment for the new residents, for the nearby commercial expansion would add several hundred jobs to the local economy.

Our congregation joined a local coalition that contacted the merchants who would locate in the mall. It negotiated their willingness to set aside a specific number of employment openings for blacks in exchange for its guaranteeing recruitment and job training, made possible through a government agency grant. Ridgefield residents were primary prospects. As a result, about thirty persons found themselves in the best work situation they had ever had and within walking distance from home at the new University Mall. Happily, businesses were beginning to realize that it was in their own best interest to employ blacks. They were learning that black customers are more likely to shop where black employees are visible, so competition to find competent employable blacks became a factor in furthering our cause.

Another need of Ridgefield families was child care. Although Binkley had operated a half-day kindergarten for some years, the nursery area remained empty during the week. A request came from members of the Chapel Hill Community Church to share sponsorship of a new daycare center. They proposed that Binkley provide space and waive utility costs while they handled all administration. Despite anxiety aired by several young mothers in the church about how the center would compromise our Sunday morning use of the same area, the congregation agreed to proceed. Soon twenty-six black infants and toddlers filled our nursery every weekday.

Although black parents from the project brought their children to the church for child care, we never saw any of them on Sundays. Yet, clearly, they knew they were welcome and that the church cared. We also tried to communicate friendship in other ways. For example, on successive Christmases we went carolling in Ridgefield and lured residents outside to join in the singing. We always persuaded a few to walk back to the church for socializing with us over hot chocolate.

When Binkley decided to cancel Sunday school during the summer months in favor of an early family-oriented service, the remainder of our education building became available for the use of older children from the project. They needed supervised activity while their parents worked. Here again, we opted for a secondary role by simply offering our classrooms, playground, and the surrounding wooded area to the Chapel Hill Department of Recreation for a day camp. Unfortunately, poor leadership resulted in such serious abuse of our building that after several seasons, the congregation withdrew from the program. In July 1971, however, another major ministry to children claimed the same space on a year-round basis. Monique LoRe, the mother of a retarded child, joined our church. She was very vocal in her advocacy for establishing what eventually became the Developmental Day Care Center for children whose mental, physical, and emotional handicaps were too severe for them to participate in a normal public school classroom. As a result, both black and white children benefited from a highly specialized program and integrated staff. The school remained at Binkley until 1978 when it needed additional space. This time a facility was provided in a renovated vacated public school building with the aid of county funds.

☙

Both of my parents died during the seventies, my mother first. Her one lung left from recurring bouts with tuberculosis finally deteriorated. As I stood by her hospital bed, she struggled to breathe and could hardly speak, but her last words to me were unmistakable in their clarity. "Take care of Rosa," she said.

Actually, Rosa was still able to care for others and remained remarkably well despite her advancing age. (She was never sure of the exact date of her birth.) She continued coming faithfully to Daddy's house just as she had always done, so for awhile my father enjoyed a continuity in his life similar to what he had been accustomed. Rosa kept everything at the house just as she knew mother would want it. She cleaned and cooked and did everything in her power to console and sustain my grieving father.

But it was not enough. Some months later he succumbed to a deep depression. Despite several long psychiatric hospitalizations and shock treatment, he never fully recovered. The best answer for his future need seemed to be placing him in the Greenwood Methodist Home where he could still see his many friends, including Rosa. Because Daddy resisted any thought of selling his home, everything remained intact there, and Rosa not only continued her care of the place but on occasion would prepare a meal there so my father could come home to spend the day.

When my father died, Pearl and I accepted the continuing responsibility for Rosa's well-being, remembering my mother's

final request. We sent monthly checks to supplement her Social
Security, and every visit to Greenwood included a visit at her
modest house which was always crowded with grandchildren.
Every time I entered Rosa's living room I had a *déjà vu* sensation, for nearly all the furnishings had come from my parents'
house as castoffs through the years. I also felt the dramatic contrast between the waning of the Old South in Greenwood and the
New South I saw emerging in Chapel Hill.

☙

Howard Lee remained mayor of Chapel Hill until 1975. He
served three consecutive terms. He was so effective that no one
even challenged him in his last election. He was, however, unable to parlay his election record to a broader base: Lee was
defeated in bids both for Congress and the lieutenant governor's
chair. Instead, he accepted an appointment in Governor James
Hunt's administration as Secretary of Natural Resources and
Community Development.

Lee's leadership in Chapel Hill was the kind of Horatio Alger
story that made good copy even in the Southern Baptist press.
His picture appeared on the front cover of the men's magazine
Brotherhood with an accompanying story that implied Lee's
election as mayor was in line with what Southern Baptists have
always supported.

A public relations pamphlet circulated by the Home Mission
Board entitled "These Southern Baptists" highlighted various
ethnic groups included in the convention and boasted, "More
than two hundred of our churches have Negro members." I
doubted the accuracy of this claim and challenged it. Home
Mission Board Secretary, Walker L. Knight, responded by refer-
ring me to several seminary professors to document the statistic,
but he admitted up front: "You have caught me in the position
of not being able to give you concrete sources from which to
readily secure definite information on the location of Southern
Baptist churches which have Negro members." The highest number I ever heard verified was twenty-nine congregations. All of
these were in such places as Alaska, or border states to the southern region, or close to university campuses.

Members of Binkley Church were outraged when the Raleigh *News and Observer* reported that newscaster Jesse Helms
had been selected by the Southern Baptist Radio and Television
Commission to receive their Lincoln Award. Many in our congregation were appalled that someone we saw as a racist could

be singled out for praise by the denomination to which we belonged. We were humiliated and embarrassed to be publicly associated with him. Jesse Helms had consistently advocated the suppression of civil liberties in situations where people had taken positions different from his own. On the race question, in particular, he had attacked every effort to secure for black citizens the same opportunities white citizens enjoy in our society.

How could this have happened? Here was a classic illustration of the simplistic attitude toward politicians that is all too common in the South. Many people judge a person to be a Christian more on the basis of personal morality than public record. For years Helms had been an active layman in Raleigh churches. He did not drink or smoke. He had never been divorced, and he and his wife had adopted a handicapped child. Few voters remembered or even cared that he successfully led the opposition to keep a black Jamaican student from joining the First Baptist Church in Raleigh. His prejudicial viewpoint dispensed daily as a television editorial did not seem to matter to voters, either. Binkley deacons authorized a strong letter of protest. They wrote, "We deeply regret that the Southern Baptist Convention, through one of its major agencies, has appeared to sanction Mr. Helms' misguided and disruptive efforts in the area of race relations." It was, however, too late for anyone to listen.

One place in Southern Baptist life where one could count on a socially conscious voice was the Christian Life Commission. During the sixties both moderates and liberals looked to this agency for encouragement and hope. Occasionally the Commission succeeded in getting its statements adopted by the Convention, but more often, unrelenting pressure forced the omission of the strongest sections. Inevitably, final versions were weakened, even though much thought was given to strategy to secure their adoption. The Christian Life Commission did well to survive under constant fire and with a minimal budget, but of course none of its final or official pronouncements were ever binding on local churches.

❦

As our nation sank deeper and deeper into the Vietnamese quagmire, the war on poverty and the war in Southeast Asia competed for the same money. Could America afford a widening foreign engagement and simultaneously fund domestic efforts to lift the poor into the nation's mainstream?

Black citizens felt mounting frustration as promised hopes

for a better life continued to elude them. The level of rising expectations led to more insistent demands for massive economic commitments, but as usual, the bottom line was money. No longer was it being requested; now blacks demanded it.

James Forman set the tone with his Black Manifesto when he seized the pulpit of the Riverside Church in New York City unexpectedly in a Sunday service. His choice of the word "reparations" gave a new sound to the civil rights movement. Repercussions were immediate and largely resentful. Southern whites reacted in their typical paternalistic mode, asking, "How could you be so rude after all we have done for you?"

A more reasoned response acknowledged the legitimacy of Forman's charge. Had not Congress introduced legislation to offer partial compensation to redress the loss of property of Japanese-Americans interned in the United States detention camps during World War II? Surely this belated gesture to return at least a token of what belonged to those victims of injustice should be a precedent for a similar appeal on behalf of American Negroes! I made a case for reparations from the pulpit, saying that restitution for injustices inflicted upon a people is an established principle of international law.

There is no doubt that our ancestors have incurred debts yet to be paid by their deprivation of black people in this land. Many of us have received our inheritance from a system that has amassed its wealth by the concerted and deliberate exploitation and underpayment of a minority race that was suppressed by both law and violence.

In Raleigh the president of Shaw University, a black school founded by Northern Baptists just after the Civil War, made an audacious appeal for $240 million to upgrade the struggling institution. Local citizens gasped at the size of the goal. When someone pointed out that the amount was larger than a similar financial campaign launched by Harvard, the Shaw president replied astutely, "Then, that means our goal is too low; surely Shaw needs twice that much!"

People were intimidated by such assertiveness. Some reacted angrily and indicated they had no intention of helping anyone who demanded it. My response was usually to remind them of what Our Lord Jesus Christ *commanded*. Any Christian who is among "the haves" is under orders to share generously with "the have-nots."

Not surprisingly, civil rights causes precipitated political conflict within ecclesiastical bodies. You would have expected this to occur within predominantly white denominations, not black ones. Yet, the national religious group to which Martin Luther King belonged offered him no support and mandated that he stop his marching. The president is credited with having accused that "those who push the doors open are sinning as much as those who bar the doors."

When political strategy failed to remove this unsympathetic leadership, King and others withdrew. Although nearby Southern Baptists saw what was happening, they remained safely silent, but other national religious groups, including American Baptists, wanted their presence felt in the South. Since it was they who had founded a large network of colleges for blacks in Dixie following the Civil War, they decided the time was ripe to renew their relationship to these institutions and thereby support students who were involved in the civil rights struggle. The person who pushed successfully for this involvement was J.C. Herrin, the chaplain who had been fired earlier at the University of North Carolina for his liberal views. Herrin became a kind of personal ambassador, riding southern highways like the Lone Ranger and extending official greetings from the northern body wherever he went.

This led eventually to the founding of American Baptist Churches of the South (ABCOTS). In Minneapolis in 1971, five thousand folk from the parent body who were gathered around an enormous Communion table welcomed these southern congregations into the denominational family. Blacks and whites embraced one another in the most memorable interracial gathering I have ever attended. Subsequently, a steady stream of outstanding black leadership entered the national body at every level like a transfusion of rich, healthy blood.

We southern whites who returned home from this mountaintop experience had high hopes that the new structure would attract an increasing number of white congregations too, but it was not to be. In the years that followed, white involvement dwindled down to a precious few, and the dream of a genuinely inclusive fellowship was deferred.

How can we account for this? Isn't it ironic that the church that was so significantly involved in furthering the civil rights agenda in southern society has not succeeded in becoming more inclusive of both races in local congregations? Indeed, blacks and whites in the South are more separated on Sunday than any other day of the week!

I am convinced that this curious situation does not have its roots in racism but rather reflects differences in culture. In their time of isolation from whites, blacks developed their own distinct type of worship, especially celebrated in their musical heritage. Also, styles of pastoral leadership took a different course. In the Old South the black preacher was one of the few persons in the black community who had managed to acquire some education, and thus, he was judged better prepared to make decisions; and since he was not altogether dependent upon whites for his upkeep, he was more free to speak. Furthermore, perceived as God's chosen spokesman, he was seldom questioned. For these reasons, southern black clergy tend to assume a more authoritarian role. Deacons are sometimes appointed by the pastor, and ministers tend to remain active far beyond their retirement years and emerge as powerful patriarchs.

In the New South, blacks are beginning to join previously all-white congregations, but very few whites seek membership in black ones. It appears that whites generally expect integration to take place on their turf, and there is a not-very-subtle implication that the blacks most acceptable to the white majority are those who have made concessions to the dominant white culture. A casual visitor at places of worship across the South today might feel that little has changed, for there are still many all-white and all-black congregations. But there is change. The sign out front that says, "Everyone Welcome" is more genuine. The "whites only" mentality is fading.

❧

The spread of black power and black separatism in the seventies throttled the zeal of many whites who up until then had been active in the civil rights struggle. When one no longer has a place on the team, one is tempted to withdraw. Some did.

The logic of separation was hard for whites to grasp. How could blacks who had paid such a high price to break out of segregation now promote separation of the races as the preferred arrangement? It seemed an unreasonable reversal of the very thing they had struggled so long to achieve.

Psychologically, however, it made sense. Blacks, who for generations had been dependent on white people, needed now to prove to themselves their ability to stand alone. On the other hand, whites, who were so accustomed to relating to blacks in condescending ways, were tempted to continue doing so even after integration had occurred. The situation was similar to that familiar stage of adolescence when a teen-ager finds it necessary to back away from parents in order to acquire a clearer sense of self-identity and to prove his or her own competence without parental assistance. Even so, the process was painful to liberal southern whites. Like parents of rebellious youth, they felt rejected and unappreciated for all they had done. It was hard to look beyond the discomfort of the moment to the future possibility of forging an even better relationship because of having had a time apart.

Black separation manifested itself in Chapel Hill when the pastors of black churches organized their own Ministerial Alliance apart from their white colleagues. White pastors protested this return to segregation but were told blacks faced special problems that were either of no concern to whites or that whites would not understand. Their judgment seemed to imply that we were either insensitive to their needs or that the races were indeed different after all. A return to separation (no longer called segregation) made the memory of the close working relationship that characterized those years of crisis look to be a smaller achievement than it had seemed. Moreover, white clergy were certain that if they had withdrawn and organized a separate white group, the black preachers would have raised "holy hell." The black clergy's separate group looked like a double standard.

The separatist movement strained Binkley's relationship to Carr Court. Neighborhood residents let it be known that white participation would no longer be needed or wanted there. They expected the church to continue its financial support, however, but with no strings attached. Their message came through like an ultimatum to test our readiness to trust them.

Members of the congregation then backed away from direct involvement as requested, but the church continued to pay the bills. Newly elected leaders in the neighborhood decided how money should be spent with no suggestions from anyone at Binkley. This appeared to be irresponsible at first, but in fact, it led to the very thing we had hoped would happen there from the outset: the emergence of competent local leadership. We admitted that we had not been altogether trusting and realized that our unhappiness over being judged dispensable reflected our need to be needed.

The Ridgefield Day Care Center presented a similar situation. Here, too, blacks wanted to be in complete charge, and the next director would be black. Administrative decisions were in the hands of an autonomous board composed mainly of parents of the black children enrolled. Although the program sometimes failed to measure up to standards that we would have chosen, we resisted the temptation to intervene because we realized that to impose those standards would have meant working against the goal of true black ownership of the operation.

❧

Black separatism is intimately related to black power. Blacks began to realize that before any ethnic group can enter an open society, it must first close ranks. To do this requires a sense of pride as well as organizational skills. "Black is beautiful" became a recurring chorus as leaders sought to project a positive image and to forge a strong sense of togetherness. It was now understood that blacks had to control their own organizations, not for the sake of excluding others, but in order to best present their own interests and be out from under paternalism. What appeared to be racism was not intended as racism. Indeed, this was in the best tradition of a healthy American pluralism. It was also a recognition of political reality in a power-driven democracy.

Power is a commodity seldom given away. It must be seized. In American society, the most effective way to do this is to go after money and votes. That is what black power is all about. The lot of black people in America will never likely improve without a redistribution of power. For too long the decisions affecting the future of blacks have been made by people of another race: in the back room, in the board room, in the skyscraper office, in the country club.

The Inter-Faith Council responded to such insights by offering staff support to a new organization of mothers who were getting public assistance called Welfare Rights. These black recipients of public funds joined hands to increase their effectiveness in calling attention to their plight. They understood that their political activity required a united voice.

Binkley offered an opportunity for members to study Saul Alinsky's controversial book *Rules for Radicals* (New York: Random House, 1971), which provided a lively forum to consider power strategy. Some of the participants felt uncomfortable at first, for Alinsky's approach is primarily confrontational. He targets the power possessor as the enemy. This approach did not sound like Christian love, yet the study group readily grasped the logic of his basic premise, that no one is likely to change his or her lot in life unless he or she has access to power. Members of the group became so intrigued by the practical wisdom articulated by Alinsky that they opted to experiment in the use of his tactics by taking on a local power base.

They selected Chapel Hill's only white funeral home, a monopoly business with no local white competition. The group's investigation revealed a refusal on the part of the management to keep inexpensive caskets on display for those who had limited means. The results of the investigation led one of the group's members to offer competition himself by building pine box coffins as an alternative to persons who preferred a simpler burial. (Incidentally, one place still securely segregated in most southern towns is the funeral home business, as is also the cemetery. Blacks and whites are seldom buried side by side.)

Another church group studied the book *Black Theology and Black Power* by James Cone (Seabury, 1969). The group members found it intensely disturbing, so much so that they requested permission to share their impressions with the entire congregation at a Sunday morning service. Such new thought arising from black America left many whites confused and called forth a flood of guilt for which no means of expiation seemed apparent.

Binkley members continued to look for ways to be responsibly involved, but now it seemed harder than ever to get a handle on the racial situation. We made overtures to the First Baptist Church whose pastor was open to finding ways of interaction. He agreed to jointly sponsor an area meeting of the American Baptist Churches of the South with each church hosting one day of the two-day meeting. He also asked that we assist First Baptist in a fund-raising event, a fashion show. Several women volunteered to participate even though this was not the kind of request anyone had anticipated. Also, our choir presented a production of the musical *1776* at the black church, where Binkley singers were warmly welcomed and much appreciated.

A further cause for concern about the racial front was what whites saw happening to their teenagers. At a time when everyone felt racism should be diminishing, racist feelings were rising at the high school. There was evidence of this among our Binkley youth, including my own children. Rightly or wrongly, white students felt reverse discrimination frequently occurred in the public schools, and they alleged that white teachers were sometimes intimidated by blacks. They accused administrators of appointing blacks to positions just because they were black, and they resented the use of quotas to insure black representation. Furthermore, they chafed under the instruction of several black teachers whom they felt were inexcusably incompetent (as were, no doubt, some white ones).

Ralph Abernathy, of the Southern Christian Leadership Conference, was once in the vicinity and spoke to a high school assembly. I could never get a reading from my children on precisely what was said, but it was clear that his coming did not make it any easier to overcome their racial feelings. Among white youth, black power and black separatism met with little understanding, only resentment.

⚕

Binkley Church became known in Chapel Hill and beyond for its political activism. It had an impressive track record in encouraging persons from the congregation to run for political office and saw this as an obvious way to make a difference in society. Conservative Baptists tend to see government as an enemy rather than a friend. They believe its primary role is to stave off evil, not to promote social welfare. Many Binkley folk had come to see that even the more traditional personal ministries might best be secured through enlightened legislation rather than through the erratic and limited responses of churches as agents of change and channels of charity.

We also gained a new understanding of the political process when we learned the hard lesson that in order to be politically effective, we must be willing to compromise. Christians who are accustomed to upholding the ideals of purity and perfection do not find it easy to settle for considerably less, nor do they want to run the risk of getting their hands soiled. We now understood that in politics one rarely gets a whole loaf and that a half loaf is better than no loaf at all.

Governor James Hunt, who was a member of Binkley Church when he was a student the UNC Law School, accepted an invitation to be the preacher of the day for a Layman's Sunday. He developed the thesis that the best way to fulfill the biblical injunction to "Love your neighbor as yourself" is to be politically active, informed about the issues, and to be responsible at the polls.

This would not be easy to do in the decade ahead.

Chapter 11

The End of an Era

As America edged toward the eighties, the civil rights movement overflowed the narrow channels of advocacy for blacks alone and began to open society to other minority groups as well. This was especially true for women and the disabled. To some lesser degree, it was also true for gays. All persons who considered themselves discriminated against in our culture learned from the racial revolution how to band together and to assert themselves.

Some of this assertiveness was directed toward the church. I still recall how startled I was when I read an article somewhere in the religious press entitled "The Woman as Nigger." Suddenly, I saw a situation to which I had been totally insensitive. It had never occurred to me that a woman's place in American culture was comparable to our keeping Negroes "in their place." The analogy hit me with convincing clarity: Women had also been relegated to a marginal involvement in American life and were by no means regarded as equals, either culturally or under the law. The white male had shaped their destiny with the very same paternalism directed toward blacks.

Binkley Church tried to move quickly to demonstrate "there is neither male nor female in Christ Jesus." As early as 1960 women were elected deacons. A woman served as moderator in 1978, and shortly thereafter the woman who had been serving as the associate in Christian education became associate pastor. All of this was done with ease. Then, in the 1980s, when we faced up to the pervasive use of masculine language in liturgy and theology, deep emotional responses sparked divisiveness.

Resistance came from two main groups. The first group was comprised mainly of literary folk who insisted there was no problem. They explained that what appeared to be sexist language was not really the case. They argued that generic words like "mankind" are by definition inclusive of both men and women. Most of the other objections were voiced by women themselves who felt no discomfort in leaving things as they were.

The changing of hymn lyrics added fuel to the fire. Some members lamented their inability to continue singing certain favorite hymns. Others felt offended if even a single sexist word was voiced anywhere in the service. As pastor, I found myself in the impossible situation of never being able to please everyone. Even though procedural policies for hymn selections were adopted by the congregation, the issue remained a constant irritant. This led to a protracted controversy at Binkley Church in a way that was never the case with the racial problem.

A more potentially explosive civil rights cause was the recognition of gays and lesbians. As pastor, of course I knew such persons in the worshiping congregation and had respected their need for privacy and protection. I felt my role was to speak forthrightly to the entire church about the discrimination suffered by homosexuals. After addressing the matter openly from the pulpit, I was amazed by the range of responses. My counseling increased sharply as I was sought out by individuals who were either struggling with their own sexual orientation or who had friends or family members who were. Also, the congregation made available the fellowship hall to the Chapel Hill Gay Rights Association for its annual banquet.

Binkley Church stumbled into a further advocacy role for a handicapped group that languishes in a disability ghetto: the deaf. A deaf couple indicated their intention to join our church. Fortunately we already had a skillful signer within the membership, Sandra Stokes, who agreed to be available at each service as their interpreter. She suggested that I learn a greeting in sign language so I could speak to them on the day they were presented to the congregation. My signs were meant to say, "I am happy to see you; welcome," but I reversed the last gesture and said "goodbye" instead! The couple has never let me forget that flub.

Eventually, Binkley had a sizable group of persons with hearing impairment, including several blacks, who became an integral part of our fellowship. The congregation affirms their presence by signing the Doxology each Sunday in worship.

In an additional effort to address the needs of the physically disabled, the Inter-Faith Council constructed twenty-two apartments with the help of federal funds. All units have wheelchair access with bath and utility fixtures designed to enable handicapped persons to care for themselves. The apartments are located conveniently near the center of Chapel Hill and are occupied by both blacks and whites.

This growing sensitivity to the civil rights of all citizens in American society is surely a direct result of the Negro's attempt to break down the barriers of segregation. In effect, black Americans have forced the nation to see the imperfections of its social order, not only in its relationship to black people but also in relationship to other groups that have endured similar discrimination, although for different reasons.

❀

The election of Ronald Reagan as president marked the end of an era. His landslide victory over Southern Baptist Jimmy Carter signaled a sharp turn to the right. It also halted Washington's commitment to the civil rights cause. Subtle racism in high places became respectable again.

Improving the plight of black America never had high priority on the new president's national agenda. If his campaign question "Are you better off now than you were four years ago?" had been asked of blacks at the close of the Reagan dynasty, the answer would have been a resounding "No." Statistics show that their economic condition either declined or hovered at about the same level for his entire time in office.

Programs meant to assist black Americans were sacrificed by the White House on the altar of militarism. Funds for health, education, and welfare suffered sharp reductions that minorities felt first. Affirmative action fell into disfavor. Even the Supreme Court chipped away at the civil rights legacy so recently achieved with rulings that compromised protection in the workplace. Housing funds earmarked for the needy ended up in the pockets of the greedy. In effect, Reagan gave privileged Americans the freedom to gratify themselves without guilt. Economic progress for blacks came to a grinding halt in the eighties. The period will be remembered for its stagnation and regresssion in addressing societal problems related to race. The political philosophy of the period was shaped in good part by the rallying cry "Ask not what

you can do for your country; ask what you can do for yourself."
The eighties were aptly called "the me generation."

These reversals in national policies were felt even in affluent
Chapel Hill. The Inter-Faith Council faced an escalating number
of clients for whom there was no safety net. Reagan's assumption that a rising tide would lift all boats proved false. The many
families in desperate financial straits forced the agency to increase its outlay of grants to more than ten thousand dollars a
month. Soon, as in nearly every other community in the country,
homeless people were walking the streets of Chapel Hill.

In 1987, I was asked by Mayor James Wallace of Chapel Hill
to chair a task force to find a location for a homeless shelter. At
that point, the Inter-Faith Council had already combed the community for more than two years—in vain. It was denied the use
of two suitable houses near the center of town because of zoning
restrictions and the usual objections of neighbors.

Meanwhile, the town of Chapel Hill had offered the old jail
in the basement of the former municipal building as a temporary
shelter. It was a damp and dingy place with cell bars still intact;
the whole building had fallen into a state of disrepair since the
new town hall had been completed. Shelter residents walked
several long blocks to the jail following dinner at the Community
Kitchen in a black neighborhood, where Inter-Faith Council
volunteers served three meals a day.

The task force continued the search for a suitable location
for the shelter, but had no better results than had the Inter-Faith
Council. Finally, only one obvious choice seemed feasible: to
stay right where we were. We had been housing the homeless in
the old jail for many months and to date no one had raised an
objection. So, we reasoned, why not move the shelter upstairs
into a renovated building and make it spacious enough to include the Community Kitchen and other related services as well?
The mayor agreed enthusiastically and promised full support.

However, when Franklin Street merchants heard our
recommendation, they moved quickly to rally opposition. They
were certain the central location would compromise the ambi-
ance of Chapel Hill, even though no complaints had been received during the two-year temporary use of the basement jail.
This group pressed for an opportunity to come up with a better
alternative. Although we had already gained the approval of the
town board to proceed as requested, we agreed to delay three
months while merchants looked for another location. In the end,
the merchants turned up nothing new.

Now, at last, the way was clear to launch the delayed capital funds drive for almost $400,000, which would be matched by community development money from the town. But in the midst of the financial campaign, we were halted once again. An ad hoc organization composed of civic leaders and elected officials, which called itself the Public Private Partnership for the improvement of Chapel Hill, had traveled to Champaign, Illinois, to compare our local planning with a comparable community. While there, a town board member raised the shelter issue again. Participants in the Partnership returned to Chapel Hill and insisted that we delay further, claiming that they were sure they could come up with a better solution. Clearly, these citizens were uncomfortable with the prospect of destitute citizens being so visible downtown. This would be an embarrassment to the community. They reasoned that some place less central would work just as well and found a site adjacent to the police station, owned by the town. Backers of this alternative promised the IFC they would raise the required funds to construct the shelter and would then deed the building to the Council.

When the Council turned down this offer, the members were accused of having closed minds. But there were two drawbacks: The site was too far for downtown street people to reach by walking, and proximity to the police station might prove intimidating to shelter clients. Persons who come to the shelter are well aware of the fact that many people see their plight as a law-and-order problem instead of an economic one. Homeless people of whatever color or condition suffer the same prejudicial stereotypes so familiar to southern blacks. Like victims of racism, they, too, are dehumanized. Their struggle for a sense of self-worth is undermined daily by society's attitude.

Finally all signals for the shelter were "go" once again. Now completed, Chapel Hill's home for the homeless is one of the best anywhere.

❦

I had considerable ambivalence about the church being expected to take up the financial slack when sources of federal money dried up. On the one hand, Christians feel compelled to ameliorate adverse conditions in every way possible, but on the other hand, to do so makes it all the easier for the government to be negligent. The Inter-Faith Council recognized the importance of its being a social action advocate in the political arena, but the task of meeting day-to-day crises and pushing the private

sector for larger outlays of charity left little energy to seek redress through government channels.

The word "freedom" began to take a backseat to the word
"equality" in civil rights circles. Some whites had thought that
once the problems of segregation had been answered by desegregation, everything else would take care of itself. It was a naive
assumption that all citizens would then be equal. This false impression probably accounts for the continuing resentment towards any people being given anything extra or receiving any
special treatment to make their way into mainstream American
life easier.

Gradually it became apparent that people trapped at the
bottom of the economic ladder would never be free unless there
were a more equitable distribution of income. It also became
clear that what had usually been seen as a racial issue was more
often an economic problem. The blacks and whites who were the
most equal were those locked in poverty together. Lines of separation were no longer drawn exclusively according to race. The
black versus white mentality began to give way to a poor versus
rich understanding.

The economic gap steadily widened during the Reagan
years with the rich getting richer and the poor becoming
poorer. According to the Center on Budget and Policy Priorities, it widened so much in the 1980s that the richest 1 percent
receive nearly as much of Americans' total income after taxes
as the bottom 40 percent! Trends in the economy trimmed the
middle class from both ends. People who prospered rose to
upper-class status while many others slipped over the edge into
poverty. In short, American society moved steadily towards a
privileged class and an underclass with whites and blacks in
both groups, though, of course, a far higher percentage of
black people has been consigned to poverty than white people.
According to the Census Bureau, white households typically
have ten times as much wealth as black households. In 1988
the median income for white families was $43,280 as compared
to $4,170 for blacks.

Martin Luther King, Jr., warned that deep economic division was just as great an evil as deep racial division. Not until this
judgment evokes a response similar to that toward racial segregation in the sixties are we likely to see dramatic change. Maybe
we should add the words "Equal at last" to King's well-known
epitaph, "Free at last."

⊗

During this period, another important agenda for Binkley Church was to provide more space for the congregation. Not only was the fellowship hall no longer large enough to accommodate further growth at worship, office space was inadquate, and there was no way to expand the Christian education program.

A long-range planning committee had researched the situation and recommended that the church build a permanent sanctuary. Then began a seemingly interminable process as members debated every conceivable alternative. For five years the church tried unsuccessfully to reach a consensus.

This plunged me into the most painful period of my pastorate. I am convinced that it is only by the grace of God that any church ever builds anything.

I fully expected objections to be raised about priorities. Commitment to outreach had always been such a primary thrust of the congregation that I knew some members would consider it immoral to invest so much money in bricks and mortar. I understood this, but I agreed with church sociologists who reasoned persuasively that a broader base in membership would in the long run provide more money for outreach than ever before. I also thought it immoral not to make room for the many new people arriving in Chapel Hill, especially in light of Binkley's choice location and ample land for further expansion.

What I was not prepared for, however, was the argument that growth threatens the life of the church and may be intrinsically bad. Some warned that growth would make the church become like a large corporation. Others said we should deliberately perpetuate our crowded conditions in order to more readily identify with the problems of population density in the Third World. Many of us were feeling somewhat uncomfortable about building spacious houses at a time when every night's news showed starving multitudes abroad. One of my associates invited persons who felt the need to combat American consumerism in favor of a simpler lifestyle to join a new support group convened at his home.

Polarization of points of view strained personal relationships. An erosion of trust ensued. Those who wanted the sanctuary accused the new lifestyle group of becoming a front to caucus against the building, while members of the lifestyle group complained when those who wanted the sanctuary were playing power politics without including the whole congregation. We sought consultation from a professor at Duke Divinity School to help us weigh our options. His suggestion, much to my dismay and disbelief, was that we divide the membership in half and become two separate congregations, using the same facility.

I endeavored to be a pastor to everyone despite the worsening situation. Those against the building felt I had compromised my ability to do so by letting my own views about the building be known, yet these were people who would have expected their pastor to take a stand on any other controversial issue.

Finally, we agreed to vote. The pro-sanctuary option overwhelmingly carried, with 85 percent of the church behind it. Everyone was exhausted by the protracted deliberations, but I promised myself to remain pastor until sufficient healing had occurred for the whole congregation to move forward together.

As with our previous building, when we simultaneously founded the Carr Court Community Center, I knew it would be spiritually healthy to launch a new social-action ministry as people pledged support for the new sanctuary. I asked a new associate who had requested exemption from fund raising to direct his energies toward involving our people in organizing a local chapter of Habitat for Humanity. Habitat houses are constructed by volunteers and made available at no interest to families seeking a way out of substandard housing. The movement began in Americus, Georgia, where most of the new home recipients are black, and it has since spread to nearly every major American city and to several continents. The Chapel Hill Comprehensive Housing Report (June 1989) notes that since 1981 the federal government has reduced its dollar commitment to housing by 75 percent. Habitat represents a small attempt on the part of the Christian community to offset this staggering reduction of available funding. Thus far in Chapel Hill, this has meant building fifteen new houses for low-income families.

❦

Another major new ministry was with prisoners, the majority of whom are black. A grim statistic that grabbed national attention recently is that one in four black American men between 20 and 29 are in prison or on parole.

The criminal justice system of the South has had a long history of violating the civil rights of black people. In the past, two standards of justice seemed to be the norm; white offenders were often dealt with less harshly than their black counterparts for the very same crime, and crimes committed by blacks against other blacks have been considered less serious than crimes committed by blacks against whites. Currently, a persuasive argument against capital punishment alleges that statistics show a greater willingness on the part of all-white southern juries to give the death sentence to blacks. This line of reasoning could lead eventually to a Supreme Court ruling abolishing the death penalty altogether.

One of Binkley's members asked the church for feasibility funds to explore the possibility of a prison ministry and contacted the director of the county prison unit to see what opportunities for involvement might be available to the congregation. Years before, our church had led services at this same prison camp on Sunday afternoons when only whites were confined there. Now blacks and whites are incarcerated together.

Our first contact with the inmates was at the prison facility, but we discovered it was possible to certify sponsors who could take the men away from the camp on outings. Bringing prisoners to worship seemed the obvious next move. Soon, on any given Sunday, a half dozen men from the unit could be found in the congregation where they were warmly welcomed.

The retired gentleman in charge of our prison ministry had an inspired idea: to take groups of inmates away for a weekend retreat with Binkley members. Conveniently, the chief chaplain of the entire state prison system, the Reverend R.A.L. Walker, was then in our church. He liked the idea and became our advocate with authorities in Raleigh who cautiously agreed to the experiment. As a result, fifteen honor-grade prisoners who wanted to participate were chosen along with an equal number of church people who volunteered to be teamed up with them for the weekend. Both men and women church members were included. We secured permission to hold the retreat at our state Baptist Camp Caraway, some distance away.

The post-retreat evaluation was positive beyond all expectations. The impact of the weekend not only changed the attitudes of those directly involved, but the whole congregation was indirectly blessed by the event. Stereotypes of both criminals and church folk were altered. The new perception reminded me of Mark Twain's famous observation that "human nature is pretty well distributed among human beings." One inmate was amazed to learn that he had shared a room at the retreat with a judge.

For two years the retreat was a line item in the outreach budget, and Binkley bore all expenses for its prisoner guests. Unfortunately, because of several serious infractions by other prisoners on released-time programs elsewhere, officials with-drew the privilege of any inmate being away from prison over-night. In subsequent years, a retreat has been held in our own church building, and the men return to camp to sleep.

The complexion of the church began to change as retirees began coming to Chapel Hill in large numbers from all over the country. One retired black couple came to us after long profes-sional careers in eastern North Carolina where they survived decades of segregated indignity. They were the first husband and wife in the history of Binkley Church to both be elected to serve as deacons on the same ballot. It has been impressive to see how they show absolutely no evidence of lasting scars from their past and seem perfectly at home now in a predominantly white social setting.

As I welcomed retirees into our congregation, I began to realize that I would soon be their peer. I knew the time had come to start my own countdown toward retirement.

❧

During this same time period—the eighties—a significant change took place in our larger church body. Fundamentalists seized control of the Southern Baptist Convention and the de-nomination turned further away from the type of social agenda Binkley had always supported.

Fundamentalists have always been the majority in Southern Baptist life, but in the past the spirit of live-and-let-live permitted conservatives, moderates, and even a few liberals to coexist. The new leadership has systematically purged from places of power every person who refuses to accept the fundamentalist position, particularly as it applies to the question of biblical inerrancy.

What happened in Southern Baptist life was a part of a much larger movement that thought of itself as the Moral Majority. Old-fashioned fundamentalism and the new political right en-tered into a symbiotic relationship. Once again pious platitudes regained popularity in the pulpit while prophetic utterances fell from grace. Politics and religion made a sharp turn to the right in concert.

I will be surprised if Southern Baptists ever return to the normalcy existing prior to the fundamentalist takeover. Al-though these recent developments are tragic, as fine institutions (especially seminaries) undergo unavoidable reshaping to con-servative specifications, I wonder if something providential could be aborning to use the situation redemptively. Already churches in the moderate Southern Baptist Alliance are admitting that they have no clout in Convention circles, nor are they likely to have any. This leaves them with two alternatives: either to form a new denomination or to become American Baptists. I pray for the latter choice. These disaffected congregations could find refuge in the very same fellowship that welcomed orphaned black congregations during the civil rights movement. They could merge with ABCOTS to become a genuinely interracial denomination, something long overdue in Dixie, a dream deferred.

❧

Jesse Jackson's rise to political stardom elicited my wholehearted admiration. To me, his career borders on the miraculous for he grew up in segregated Greenville, South Carolina, very close to my own birthplace in Greenwood. I am amazed that he has transcended the deprivation and prejudice of his childhood. When Jesse addressed the 1988 Democratic Convention and described poverty in America with the recurring phrase "I understand," I, too, understood. We are products of the same culture, only Jesse came from the other side of the tracks; I was privileged and he was poor.

When Jackson visited Chapel Hill seeking support for his Rainbow Coalition, I welcomed an invitation to sit with him on the stage. In fact, I felt an almost mystical kinship with him, as if we were truly brothers. He drew a large audience in the university gymnasium. The majority of those present were black, but the crowd looked like salt and pepper from the podium.

Black power had become a force to be reckoned with in the national Democratic Party. Who would have thought during those early days of the civil rights movement that a black from South Carolina could emerge so soon as a serious power broker, if not contender, for the White House! Even Jesse Helms saw the handwriting on the wall and added a black man to his staff, a Morehead Scholar graduate of the University of North Carolina.[1] More typically, however, Helms still protests the holiday observance of Martin Luther King, Jr.'s birthday by making every member of his staff show up for work on that day as usual.

Despite incredible progress, racism persists in the South's political cauldron. I cannot forget a conversation overheard on the porch of a resort hotel near the Georgia border. A fashionably dressed lady was talking to a couple from Atlanta to whom she asked, "What's the name of your famous black legislator down there?"

"You mean Julian Bond?" the Atlantan answered.

"Yes," the woman replied. "Can't you all find somebody down there to shoot him?"

🌀

Our racism extends to South Africa. I was surprised to learn that my own bank, the North Carolina National Bank (NCNB), was one of the largest American investors in the apartheid economy. Since I then owned a sliver of NCNB stock, I took advantage of my prerogative to attend the annual stockholders meeting in Charlotte. American Baptists wanted representation there to protest the bank's large South African holdings. As it turned out, there was no necessity for me to speak, for several blacks had been given proxies by American Baptists and made impassioned statements. Two years later, in 1988, NCNB responded to the pressure from black customers and began to change its policy.

Upon learning that Bishop Desmond Tutu of South Africa would be speaking in Duke Chapel, I felt some word of welcome from local Baptists would be timely. Jerry Falwell, an independent Baptist, had just returned from South Africa and said to the press that Tutu was a phony. I joined with Bill Finlator, the prophetic former minister of the Pullen Memorial Baptist Church of Raleigh, in signing a statement to assure Tutu that Falwell did not speak for us.

🌀

Gradually, the racial issue was supplanted by the peace issue as the primary social concern of the American church. Congregations were finding it increasingly difficult to get a handle on the racial issue as it manifested itself in more diffuse ways: deepening poverty for the unskilled, increasing high-school dropout rates, drug abuse, and teen-age pregnancy. Now the threat of a nuclear holocaust and the cost of the military build-up began to overshadow everything else. Not only the Cold War but also the civil wars in Central America cried out for attention. Church people sometimes assumed that the civil rights battles at home had been won; now the peace issue demanded priority.

In Chapel Hill, a Fellowship to Reverse the Arms Race was called into being by the Chapel Hill clergy. The organization expended considerable energy trying to find responsible ways to further its stated purpose. Eventually it merged with several similar groups to become a part of the North Carolina Center for Peace. Concurrently, Binkley Church responded to a request to participate in a Soviet-American citizens' exchange, sponsored by Bridges for Peace. Funds were designated to put the cost within reach of those who wanted to go. Their reports back to the congregation humanized the peace issue and put government policy in an altogether different perspective.

A delegation of Russian visitors came to Chapel Hill in 1987 to reciprocate the recent trip of Chapel Hillians to their country. One Russian was a Baptist pastor who participated in our Sunday morning service, and his warm pastoral greeting evoked an unprecedented emotional response from our people. Another Soviet visitor who had traveled across North Carolina told reporters how surprised he was not to find a single person in the state who favored segregation! Obviously, this is not the kind of thing one would likely admit to a Russian.

If the level of trust between our two countries continues to rise, the resources saved by a reduction in military appropriations could be spent for social welfare. The gap separating our underclass from the rest of American society could be closed. Only generous funding for education and economic opportunity is likely to make the necessary difference. Civil rights access alone will never suffice. In his remarkable speech at Howard University as far back as 1965, President Lyndon Johnson said, "the next and more profound stage of civil rights" must be an economic Reconstruction.

❧

In the final years of my pastorate at Binkley Church, I felt very much a part of the whole community, no longer on the periphery. In the church, stress about the building project and the use of sexist language began to lessen. I felt affirmed again by those who had distanced themselves from me during the past controversy. Signs of emerging good health were evident in every part of the church body. My long tenure had begun to pay special dividends of pleasure in seeing families through a whole lifecycle. Children whose births I had welcomed were now bringing their own children to the church to be dedicated.

My own Robert and Frances also crossed that magic line called maturity. They gave no indication of having suffered serious harm for having had a largely absentee father.

My friendships with black persons continued to bless my

life. I accepted an invitation to preach at a large black church in Augusta, Georgia. I returned home via Wheeler Air Lines, a small commuter company owned and operated by a black family from Durham. I found myself the only passenger on board with a black pilot at the controls. As we flew over South Carolina, I was amused to wonder what my grandfather might think if he could have seen me then. Surely, he would have concluded that I had a Negro chauffeur for my heavenly chariot!

I continue to be grateful for a conversation at a surprise birthday dinner that Howard Lee gave for his wife, Lillian. Pearl and I were the only white couple present; all of the other guests were black. As the evening progressed, the wine flowed freely. A friend across the table may have been feeling the effects of the libations, but I shall never forget what he said to me that evening: "Bob, you're not white; you're black. You're one of us." Seldom have I felt so fully accepted.

❧

I announced my retirement on the first Sunday of January, 1988, as I was about to enter my thirtieth year as pastor of Binkley Church. In those final months, I sought to prepare the congregation for the approaching transition. Nearly every Sunday, former members came back to visit, including a black family who traveled all the way from Buffalo, New York.

My last sermon fell on Pentecost. This afforded a ready-made opportunity to reflect upon the past and to remember the many evidences of God's Spirit empowering us. On the following Sunday, at my retirement service, I sat in the congregation on the front row with my family beside me. Denton Lotz, general secretary of the Baptist World Alliance, preached the sermon. His text was that same Micah reference (6:8) engraved over the entrance to Gerrard Hall, the place of Binkley Church's beginning: "What does the Lord require of you, but to do justice, and to love kindness, and to walk humbly with your God?"

It was a joyful celebration and a time of warm thanksgiving. As we stood to sing the last hymn, I turned around to get a quick glimpse of the congregation behind me. My glimpse locked into an astonished stare. I saw Rosa walking slowly down the aisle.

My voice constricted. I could sing no longer. I felt my life had come full circle.

Afterword

The church made a contribution of $10,000 to the new community shelter in my name and established an endowed symposium on "The Role and Responsibility of the Christian Church in Today's World" as a way of remembering my ministry.

Pearl retired from her position as organist six months after I did, wanting everyone to understand that she had been a staff person in her own right. She also wanted an extension of time to enjoy playing the magnificent new pipe organ that the congregation had installed in her honor only a year before. On her final Sunday, she was presented with a gold key to the console of the Pearl Frances Seymour Organ to which she could now have access at any time she liked.

☙

Several months after retiring, I was invited to attend the installation service of the new senior minister of the Riverside Church in New York City, which had been made famous by its first distinguished pastor, Harry Emerson Fosdick. The person named for that prestigious pulpit was the Reverend James Forbes, the same young black man who had his first experience in ministry as an intern at Binkley Church in the early sixties! Today he is regarded as one of the most outstanding pulpiteers in America.

He invited me to process with the celebrants as a special guest, so I determined to be there. The overflowing black-white congregation was accented by bright red liturgical robes. Just before his first official act as pastor at the close of the service, Forbes delayed the benediction to make a few personal remarks. He recognized several friends who had played a vital role in his life. He introduced me as his first colleague in ministry and the pastor who had performed his marriage ceremony. "Old times there are not forgotten . . . look away, Dixieland!"

✿

Soon after retirement I was invited to preach at the First Baptist Church of Greenwood. The stately new Gothic structure stands directly across the street from where I lived as a child. I was surprised to find so many familiar faces in the congregation, many of whom were friends of my parents. They received me warmly and with a sense of pride recalled having ordained me to ministry almost a half-century ago. I feel a deep debt of gratitude for the dear people who nurtured me there. My parents are remembered at First Baptist by an endowed discretionary fund to meet the personal needs of individuals in crisis, many of whom are black.

✿

Charlotte has become a major American city. The Myers Park Baptist Church is now housed in a magnificent Colonial-style building, complete with box pews. The church speaks to the growing metropolis with a relevant and respected voice. The state president of the NAACP, Kelly Alexander, has said of Charlotte, "The housing barriers are set by what you can afford, not the color of your skin."[1] The city is far less segregated than many northern ones.

Its former black mayor, Harvey Gantt, won the Democratic senatorial primary and contended against Jesse Helms in his bid for reelection. Although Gantt was defeated, 35 percent of the white voters of North Carolina gave him their support, and Helms felt genuinely threatened by the contest. Predictably, in the final days of the campaign Helms played the race card, but the outcome clearly indicated that racial considerations are gradually being pushed aside by the voters of North Carolina. Shortly thereafter, Dan Blue, a state legislator who is also black, was easily elected to serve as the speaker of the House of Representatives. This cushioned the pain of Gantt's failure to defeat Jesse by putting a black politician in a highly visible and influential office. Also, Chapel Hill's Howard Lee won a seat in the state Senate.

❦

I went to Warrenton for a day's visit with former parishioners. I was pleased to hear that the private school that was founded to circumvent integration was forced to close for lack of adequate funds and too few students. Now all blacks and whites attend the public school together.

The Warrenton Country Club is still for whites only. It even excludes a new physician and his family from India who have settled in the community to offer a medical practice to the county. As persons of color, they suffer the consequences of a stubborn tradition.

Warren County is where Floyd McKissick tried to establish Soul City, which was to have been a model community for blacks. Despite the millions of federal dollars poured into the project, it, too, remains another dream deferred.

❦

Mars Hill College tapped me for a further term as a trustee. I delivered the Founders Day address in the fall of 1989. The occasion had heightened significance for me since this was also the time of the premiere of a film produced for the college about Old Joe, who was jailed as security against the school's early indebtedness. Joe's great-great-granddaughter, Oralene Graves, who was the first black student admitted to the college, now has a daughter of her own in the student body. Today Mars Hill College has a higher percentage of black students in the student body than does any institution of higher learning in western North Carolina, either public or private. Sixty black young people are enrolled.

❦

I am pleased that both of my children have become a part of a new generation to whom racial considerations are incidental and of no significant consequence. Frances is the program director for the Ford Foundation in Indonesia where her husband also works with the World Bank. (I call them my secular missionaries.) Recently, the distinguished black leader Vernon Jordan, now a trustee of the Foundation, was a guest in their home.

Our son, Rob, has completed a residency in anesthesiology

at the Baptist Hospital in Winston-Salem. I tease him about upholding the family tradition of putting people to sleep. He was assigned a job rotation in a Philadelphia hospital at a time when I was making frequent trips to the American Baptist headquarters in Valley Forge, and I stayed with him once overnight. The next morning he said he would be picked up by a friend with whom he was car pooling to work. The friend turned out to be a young black physician, also from North Carolina.

A call from Greenwood informed us that Rosa was critically ill. She had broken a hip and was a patient at the Self Memorial Hospital. Weeks passed with little evidence of improvement even though she was getting excellent care from both white and black nurses in the integrated medical complex. We realized she might be dying.

Pearl and I drove to Greenwood in response to her weakened voice on the telephone, saying, "Please come." As I stood by her bedside, holding her hand, I remembered a conversation with Rosa from almost sixty years ago, when I was a child.

After her cabin behind our house burned, Rosa moved with her family to another place not far away. The shortest route to this house was through a large cemetery, and she would walk it day or night. I asked her, "Aren't you afraid to walk through the cemetery after dark?" She said, "No, chile, you're not afraid to go through the cemetery when you know your home is on the other side." Several months later, Rosa died. I was the only white face at the funeral. I was listed in the obituary with her children as her "guardian son."

I feel exceedingly fortunate for my life's coinciding with the racial revolution and for the privilege of having had a part in the civil rights movement. I still am not accustomed to the dramatic changes I see all around me. Indeed, I become quite emotional when I see a black person in a role I would never have dreamed possible such a short time ago. Evidences of the new culture affect me with amazement and fill me with gratitude. I cannot imagine what it would be like to grow up in the South today and take all that has happened for granted.

While everyone else at the Carolina basketball game is responding to the appeal of the cheerleaders to make more noise, I am looking not at the blue and white but at the black and white. When a white female cheerleader sits on the shoulders of the black male cheerleader, I recall days when such innocent physical contact could have led to a lynching.

I get distracted from the menu in restaurants when I notice black customers seated at nearby tables. I still find myself surprised to see them there. I am shocked when I travel down east and stop for barbecue at what was once a redneck kind of place and see white and black teen-agers waiting on tables together as equals.

I choke up when I hear news of a Ron Brown being chosen to head the National Democratic Party, or when I learn that the new chief of staff of the armed forces of our nation is black. When Douglas Wilder was elected governor of Virginia, I was greatly moved. The contrast between this stately gentleman and the traditional stereotype that inspired "Carry me back to ole Virginny; dat's where this ole darky's heart am longed to go," is overwhelming.

The increasing pride of southerners in the New South reminds me of a similar situation in United States history when American women were struggling to secure the right to vote. When the first parade in support of the controversial proposal was held in New York City, forty-seven men were brave enough to march with the women. After the constitutional amendment guaranteeing the franchise to women was finally passed, another parade was planned to celebrate their victory. Invitations went out to all of those men who had marched in that first demonstration. When the appointed day arrived, all 508 of the original forty-seven men were on hand to participate! After the victory had been won, everyone wanted to claim credit for having been on the front line.

Something similar to this is occurring in the South today. Now that society is becoming inclusive, nearly everyone agrees that the change is for the better. Some people are tempted to rewrite history and to see themselves as having been more active in the civil rights movement than they actually were. After experiencing the first breath of spring, no one wants to be remembered as someone who preferred the long, bitter winter.

> Cry aloud the great proclamation.
> Join the cause of love and liberation.
> There will be some changes made.
> We're ready to be led now,
> The drums are up ahead now;
> Love is on the way.[2]

Notes

Introduction
1. Eldridge Cleaver, "Why I Left America, and Why I Am Returning," *The New York Times* (September 30, 1990).

Chapter 1
1. Bruce Catton, *This Hallowed Ground* (Garden City: Doubleday, 1956), p. 222.
2. "America the Possible," by Anthony Lewis, *The New York Times*, 24 July 1988. Copyright © 1988 by The New York Times Company. Reprinted by permission.
3. Words from "The Battle Hymn of the Republic" by Julia Ward Howe.

Chapter 2
1. Countee Cullen, "For a Lady I Know" from *On These I Stand* by Countee Cullen. Copyright 1925 by Harper & Row, Publishers, Inc., renewed 1953 by Ida M. Cullen. By permission of Harper & Row, Publishers, Inc.

Chapter 3
1. Gunnar Myrdal, *An American Dilemma* (New York: Harper & Bro., 1944), p. 873.

Chapter 4
1. Jan Struther, "Wartime Journey" from *The Glass Blower and Other Poems* by Jan Struther. Copyright 1943 by Jan Struther. By permission of Curtis Brown, Ltd.

Chapter 5
1. Words from "Let Us Break Bread Together," an American spiritual.

Chapter 8
1. Twenty-five years later, the staff director of the SCEF conference, Anne Braden, received the first Americanism Award from the American Civil Liberties Union.
2. Words from "In Christ There Is No East or West" by John Oxenham, 1852–1941. By permission of Desmond Dunkerley.

Chapter 9
1. Lillian Smith, *Killers of the Dream* (W. W. Norton & Company, 1949), p. 220.

Chapter 11
1. This person was later replaced by James Meredith who, as a student, became famous for his single-handed attempt to integrate the University of Mississippi.

Afterword
1. *Newsweek*, (February 6, 1989).
2. Words from "Join the Revolution" by Richard Avery and Donald Marsh. Copyright © 1970 by Hope Publishing Co., Carol Stream, IL 60188. All rights reserved. Used by permission.